MILE BY MILE
London to Paris

Mile by Mile

LONDON TO PARIS

The entire railway journey by
historic Golden Arrow and modern Eurostar
mapped for the interested traveller

Maps by Reginald Piggott
Text and research by Matt Thompson

First published in Great Britain 2012
by Aurum Press Ltd
7 Greenland Street, London NW1 0ND
www.aurumpress.co.uk

Every effort has been made to trace the copyright holders of material
quoted in this book. If application is made in writing to the publisher,
any omissions will be included in future editions.

A catalogue record for this book is available from the British Library.

ISBN 978 1 84513 772 4

1 3 5 7 9 10 8 6 4 2
2012 2013 2015 2014 2013

This book is printed on paper certified by the Forest Stewardship
Council as coming from a forest that is well managed according
to strict environmental, social and economic standards.

Design by Tim Peters
Printed by MPG Books, Bodmin, Cornwall

CONTENTS

Matt Thompson has studied the railways of Great Britain
and tourist guidebooks for several years and has carried out extensive
research into the ways that railways marketed the destinations
that they served.
He is based in the great railway centre of York and, from there, makes
forays into the wider world with dogs and family in tow.

Reginald Piggott was born in Leamington Spa in 1930. Both
his grandfathers were lifelong railwaymen, as driver and signalman
respectively. Reg started work at 13 in a large booksellers,
later becoming a lecturer at Leicester College of Art & Technology,
specialising in paleography and cartography, and retired
from map-making at the age of 81.

Together they collaborated on the GWR section of the first
Mile by Mile book in homage to S. N. Pike, also published by Aurum.
The present book addresses the legendary rail routes from
London to Paris in the same idiom.

INTRODUCTION

The idea of a tunnel connecting Great Britain with France goes back at least to 1802. It would take almost another 200 years for this dream to come true and for a passenger to be able to board a train in London and arrive in Paris without ever having to leave their seat.

In 1994, the Channel Tunnel was opened and suddenly Great Britain was connected to the continent by the Eurostar in a way that was seen as a curse to some and a blessing to others. But the railways of Great Britain had been moving people across the Channel to France for almost 150 years before this, most notably with the stylish Golden Arrow service that, during its inter-war heyday, added a touch of luxury to what had previously been something of an uncomfortable voyage.

This book is designed to act as an armchair guide to the routes of the Eurostar and Golden Arrow. Of course, that armchair could well be on a train. It would be a perfect companion on a trip to Paris and be able to tell you things about the landscapes and locations through which you passed at such a dizzying speed but it would also serve those who like their travel a little closer to home.

It tells the story of the two main routes between London and Paris separated by 60 years and a second World War. With it, you can lose yourself in the orchards of Kent or the farmland of Picardy. The towns and villages through which you pass (either in your mind or in reality) are gone so quickly that they can feel empty or without character; they are just a blur in the empty space between one's starting point and one's destination. The aim of this book is to bring back some of the character and individuality to these places and to recreate the adventure of a bygone era.

km ← miles **UNIT** km → miles

km ← miles	UNIT	km → miles
1.61	1	0.62
3.22	2	1.24
4.83	3	1.86
6.43	4	2.48
8.04	5	3.10
9.65	6	3.73
11.26	7	4.35
12.87	8	4.97
14.48	9	5.59
16.10	10	6.21
24.10	15	9.31
32.18	20	12.42
40.23	25	15.03
48.28	30	18.64
56.27	35	21.74
64.37	40	24.85
72.41	45	27.96
80.46	50	31.07
88.51	55	34.17
96.56	60	37.28
104.60	65	40.37
112.65	70	43.49
120.70	75	46.60
128.75	80	49.71
136.79	85	52.81
144.84	90	55.92
152.88	95	59.02
160.93	100	62.13

Conversions approximate to second decimal place

Conversion table for distances. Miles to km and km to miles
(for km, multiply miles x 1.609; for miles, multiply km x 0.621)

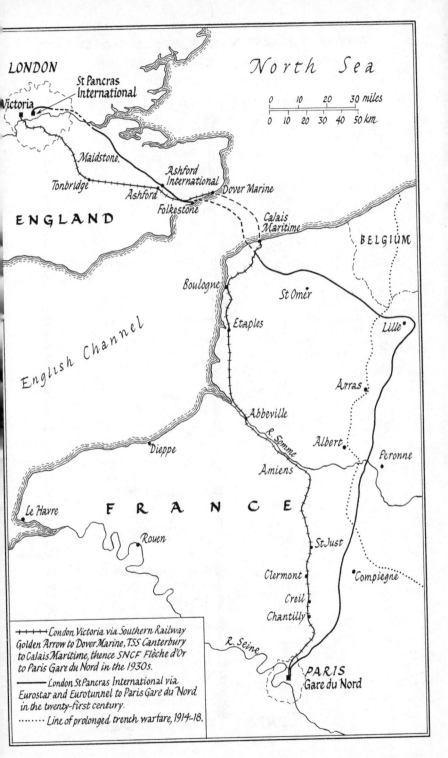

North Sea

LONDON

St Pancras
International

Victoria

Maidstone

Tonbridge

Ashford
International

Ashford

Folkestone

Dover Marine

Calais
Maritime

ENGLAND

BELGIUM

Boulogne

St Omer

Lille

English Channel

Etaples

Arras

Abbeville

R. Somme

Albert

Dieppe

Peronne

Amiens

Le Havre

FRANCE

Rouen

St Just

Clermont

Compiegne

Creil

Chantilly

R. Seine

PARIS
Gare du Nord

+++++ London Victoria via Southern Railway
Golden Arrow to Dover Marine, TSS Canterbury
to Calais Maritime, thence SNCF Flèche d'Or
to Paris Gare du Nord in the 1930s.

——— London St Pancras International via
Eurostar and Eurotunnel to Paris Gare du Nord
in the twenty-first century.

.... Line of prolonged trench warfare, 1914–18.

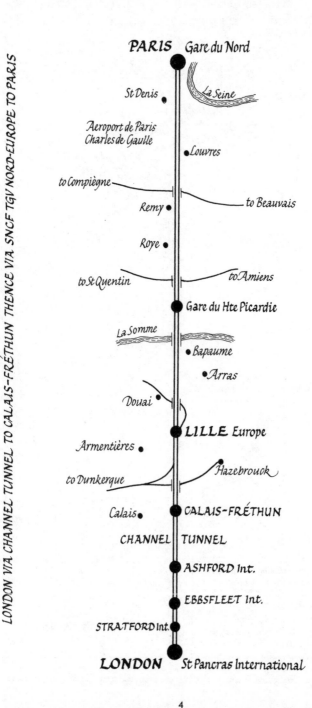

PRINCIPAL STATIONS ON THE GOLDEN ARROW—FLÈCHE D'OR ROUTE

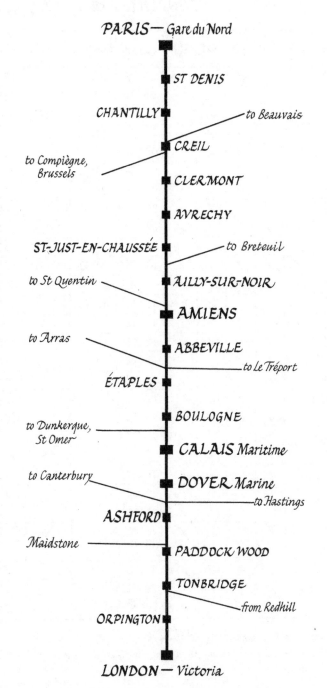

PARIS— Gare du Nord

ST DENIS

CHANTILLY

CREIL — to Beauvais

to Compiègne, Brussels

CLERMONT

AVRECHY

ST-JUST-EN-CHAUSSÉE — to Breteuil

to St Quentin — AILLY-SUR-NOIR

AMIENS

to Arras — ABBEVILLE

to Le Tréport

ÉTAPLES

BOULOGNE

to Dunkerque, St Omer

CALAIS Maritime

to Canterbury — DOVER Marine

to Hastings

ASHFORD

Maidstone — PADDOCK WOOD

TONBRIDGE

from Redhill

ORPINGTON

LONDON — Victoria

From CALAIS CHEMIN DE FER DU NORD (NORTHERN RAILWAY OF FRANCE)

LONDON to PARIS via AMIENS = 463 kilometres or 288 miles

SOUTHERN RAILWAY to DOVER

MON	TUE	WED	THU	FRI	SAT	SUN	London	Ebbsfleet	Ashford	Paris	Train No.
✓	✓	✓	✓	✓	·	·	05:25	05:42		08:50	9078
·	·	·	·	·	✓	·	06:22	·		09:47	9002
✓	✓	✓	✓	✓	✓	·	06:52	·	07:25	10:17	9004
✓	✓	✓	✓	✓	✓	·	07:22	07:41		10:47	9006
✓	✓	✓	✓	✓	✓	·	08:02	·		11:17	9008
·	·	·	·	·	✓		08:26	08:42		11:47	9010
✓	✓	✓	✓	·	·	·	08:55	09:12		12:17	9012
·	·	·	·	·	✓	·	09:00	·	·	12:17	9012
✓	✓	✓	✓	✓	✓	✓	09:22	·	09:55	12:47	9014
✓	✓	✓	✓	✓	·	·	10:00	·	·	13:17	9016
✓	✓	✓	✓	✓	✓	✓	10:25	10:42		13:47	9018
✓	✓	✓	✓	✓	✓	✓	11:01	·	·	14:17	9020
·	·	·	·	·	✓	·	11:25	11:42		14:47	9022
·	·	·	·	✓	·	·	11:32	·		14:47	9022
✓	✓	✓	✓	✓	✓	✓	12:28	12:45		15:50	9024
·	·	·	✓	·	·	·	13:00	·	·	16:17	9026
·	·	·	·	·	·	✓	13:02	·	·	16:17	9026
✓	✓	✓	✓	✓	·	✓	14:02	·	·	17:23	9030
✓	✓	✓	✓	✓	·	✓	15:02	·	·	18:17	9034
·	·	·	·	·	✓	✓	15:32	·	·	18:47	9036
✓	✓	✓	✓	✓	·	·	16:02	·	·	19:17	9038
✓	✓	✓	✓	✓	✓	✓	16:22	·	16:55	19:47	9040
✓	✓	✓	✓	✓	·	·	17:30	·		20:47	9044
·	·	·	·	·	✓	✓	17:32	·	·	20:47	9044
✓	✓	✓	✓	✓	·	✓	18:02	·	·	21:17	9046
·	·	·	·	✓	·	·	18:32	·	·	21:47	9048
✓	✓	✓	✓	✓	✓	✓	19:02	·	·	22:17	9050
✓	✓	✓	✓	✓	✓	✓	20:02	·	·	23:17	9054
·	·	·	·	·	·	✓	20:32	·	·	23:47	9056

Note that times of arrival in Paris are European time.

124 trains per week on Eurostar compared to no more than half-a-dozen in the 1930s.

LONDON to PARIS Summer 1930 & Winter 1930–31
Dover—Calais route

Outwards		1st Class Luxe	1st & 2nd Class	1st, 2nd & 3rd Cl.
London Victoria	dep.	11:00	11:15	16:00
Dover Marine	arr.	12:38	12:53	17:38
	dep.	12:55	13:15	17:55
Calais Maritime	arr.	14:10	14:30	19:15 1st & 2nd Cl.
	dep.	14:25	15:06	19:50
Paris du Nord	arr.	17:35	R 18:23	A R 23:15

('Golden Arrow Limited' in 1st Class Luxe column)

A 1st Class Pullman Car between Calais and Paris
R Restaurant Car between Calais and Paris

Inwards		1st & 2nd Class	1st Class Luxe	1st & 2nd Class
Paris du Nord	dep.	10:00 A R	12:00	12:15 R
Calais Maritime	arr.	13:15 1st, 2nd & 3rd Cl.	15:10	15:30
	dep.	13:40	15:25	15:55
Dover Marine	arr.	15:00	16:40	17:10
	dep.	15:30	16:57	17:35
London Victoria	arr.	17:15	18:35	19:15

('Golden Arrow Limited' in 1st Class Luxe column)

Times according to the 24-hour clock
A 1st Class Pullman Car between Paris and Calais
R Restaurant Car between Paris and Calais

TIMETABLE

Victoria and St Pancras

The journey from London to Paris on board the Eurostar begins at the iconic St Pancras station. A striking combination of modern design and sculpture alongside the High Gothic style of the 1860s help make this station a vibrant and exciting place to be, although it has not always been so well thought of and at one point, only narrowly escaped demolition.

In the 1860s, the Midland Railway began to purchase land in the parish of St Pancras in the north of London. While the train sheds were designed by the Midland Railway's own architects, George Gilbert Scott was appointed architect of the hotel, the Midland Grand, that was built at the front of the terminus. In 1864, work began.

The building site contained two graveyards from local churches and the River Fleet and these obstacles had to be negotiated. The design for the buildings was sophisticated and took into account the type of goods that were going to be stored and later transported around the country. The famous vaulted cellar, or undercroft, on which the station stands was designed on a grid system based on the standard size of the Burton beer barrels that the Midland Railway moved down from Staffordshire.

In 1868 the station was completed; the hotel deliberately designed to outshine the classical lines of Euston station and the more dour appearance of King's Cross. The grand Gothic style certainly made an impact although, as time went on, it was seen as unfashionable and dated. By the 1920s, St Pancras had been sidelined in favour of nearby Euston. This began the trend of underuse and subsequent dereliction that was to continue, on and off, for the rest of the twentieth century. In the 1930s, the Midland Grand Hotel became too costly to run, was closed to the public and transformed into offices for the railway company.

In 1962, it seemed likely that St Pancras would be demolished but with the backing of popular figures such as Sir John Betjeman and Sir Nikolaus Pevsner, the buildings were finally saved from demolition and given listed status in 1967.

The station continued to be in use but the buildings went into further decline and in the 1980s they were considered too dangerous to use. However, there were plans ahead to renovate the station and its buildings and to use them as the terminus for the new Eurostar service from London to Paris. In April 2004, the original train shed closed to railway traffic and work began on renovating the station. HM Queen Elizabeth II officially opened the rebuilt St Pancras International station on 6 November 2007.

If one were to leave for Paris, on board the Golden Arrow, in the 1930s the starting point of the journey would have been Victoria station. This station had complex beginnings but was first suggested in the late 1850s. By 1862, the station had opened but was, in reality, two stations: one run by the London, Chatham and Dover Railway (LCDR), and shared with the Great Western, and the other run by the London, Brighton and South Coast Railway (LBSCR). While the stations were side by side, they had separate entrances and two independent station masters.

The station plays a brief, if entertaining, part in Oscar Wilde's play, *The Importance of Being Earnest*, when Jack tells Lady Bracknell that he was found with a handbag in the cloakroom at Victoria station (more specifically, on the Brighton side), leading to Lady Bracknell's exclamation, 'A handbag?'

The different sides of the station were rebuilt at different times as the two companies vied with each other for prestige. In 1881, the first all-Pullman trains left the LBSCR side as the Pullman Limited, which took passengers in luxury from London to Brighton. The South Eastern and Chatham Railway (SECR) side was completely remodelled in the early part of the twentieth century in a grand Edwardian style.

This separate status changed in 1923, when both railway companies came under the ownership of the Southern Railway. At this time the wall that divided the two stations was breached and the platforms were renumbered consecutively, making Victoria station whole after more than 60 years divided.

The Golden Arrow was to be one of the most famous services to leave from Victoria and although there were many changes in the timetable and stoppages during the Second World War, it continued to depart from here until the last service on 30 September 1972. The station is now perhaps better known as a bus terminal, although it remains a busy London station that sees more than 70 million users every year.

Opposite: Penny train arriving at Victoria Station, 1865
Above: The interior of St Pancras Station, 1883

About 10 km outside St Pancras the line passes Stratford International station. The building itself was completed in 2006 although the station was not opened until November 2009. Originally built as a regular station stop for the Eurostar, an early review of the service suggested that stopping a high-speed train just seven minutes after beginning its journey was not ideal and services were withdrawn. However, with the 2012 Olympic Park and Village so nearby and the planned regeneration of East London, there was strong opposition to this. While the Eurostar continues to pass through this station without stopping, other train operators have expressed an interest in making use of it for continental services, including one to the German city of Frankfurt.

Throughout the period of the Olympics a service known as the *Olympic Javelin* will make use of the station to bring people from central London and the Eurostar station at Ebbsfleet.

After pulling away from St Pancras International the train makes its way through central London. It passes under the vibrant areas of Islington and Bethnal Green to the right. Minutes later the train passes under Hackney Marshes. This marshland was extensively drained from the medieval period and an inn, The White House, was reputedly a haunt of the highwayman Dick Turpin. The marshes now provide vital open space for recreation and are also an important wildlife habitat. However, areas of the marsh have recently been extensively developed for the London Olympic Park.

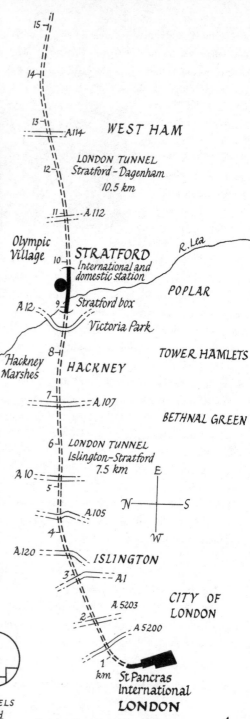

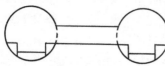

LONDON AND THAMES TUNNELS
Twin bore single track, connected

Distance markers are in kilometres

1a

10

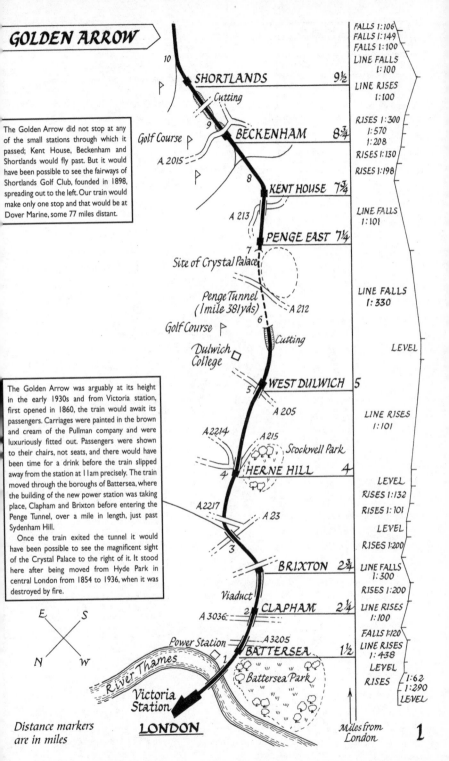

GOLDEN ARROW

The Golden Arrow did not stop at any of the small stations through which it passed; Kent House, Beckenham and Shortlands would fly past. But it would have been possible to see the fairways of Shortlands Golf Club, founded in 1898, spreading out to the left. Our train would make only one stop and that would be at Dover Marine, some 77 miles distant.

The Golden Arrow was arguably at its height in the early 1930s and from Victoria station, first opened in 1860, the train would await its passengers. Carriages were painted in the brown and cream of the Pullman company and were luxuriously fitted out. Passengers were shown to their chairs, not seats, and there would have been time for a drink before the train slipped away from the station at 11am precisely. The train moved through the boroughs of Battersea, where the building of the new power station was taking place, Clapham and Brixton before entering the Penge Tunnel, over a mile in length, just past Sydenham Hill.

Once the train exited the tunnel it would have been possible to see the magnificent sight of the Crystal Palace to the right of it. It stood here after being moved from Hyde Park in central London from 1854 to 1936, when it was destroyed by fire.

Distance markers are in miles

11

EUROSTAR

About 25 km from St Pancras the train passes through Rainham Marshes. Like Hackney Marshes, this area has a long history although it has not been as extensively drained and retains much of its original character. The site had been a military firing range for over a century but opened as a nature reserve in 2006 and is now considered to be an important wildlife habitat. The marshes sustain numerous bird species such as lapwing, little egret, bearded tit and peregrine falcon.

Excavations carried out when building the High Speed 1 have shown that the area was occupied in the Mesolithic Period, some 8,000 years ago. Flint tools suggest that people hunted the fish, wildfowl and animals that lived in the wetlands.

Purfleet

30

A 1099

LONG REACH

R. Darent

Industrial Estate

KENT

ESSEX

25

Rainham Marshes

RSPB Reserve

River Thames

A 13

A 1306

Industrial Estate

Motor Works

DAGENHAM

THAMESMEAD

Container Terminal

20

Barking Reach

The line now passes into Essex and crosses and re-crosses the main A13 road while, at the same time, following the River Thames. Just over 20 km from St Pancras the line passes by the Ford Dagenham car plant, which can be recognised by the two wind turbines that have been built on the site. These turbines are 85 metres high and comprised the first 'wind farm' to be built in London. From the beginnings of the plant, in the 1930s, it has produced over 10 million Ford cars. Work at the site has changed dramatically over the past few years and cars are no longer assembled there, however it is still a busy manufacturing site building car engines. Much of the material that the plant needed was transported, not by rail, but along the River Thames.

Cars on the railway network were more common than one might first suppose. From the mid-1950s British Rail transported travellers' cars on the railway with their Motorail system. While this had all but been ended by privatisation, there were still some services operating until the mid-2000s.

E

N —— S

W

Barking Creek

Tunnel

Works

Docks

2a

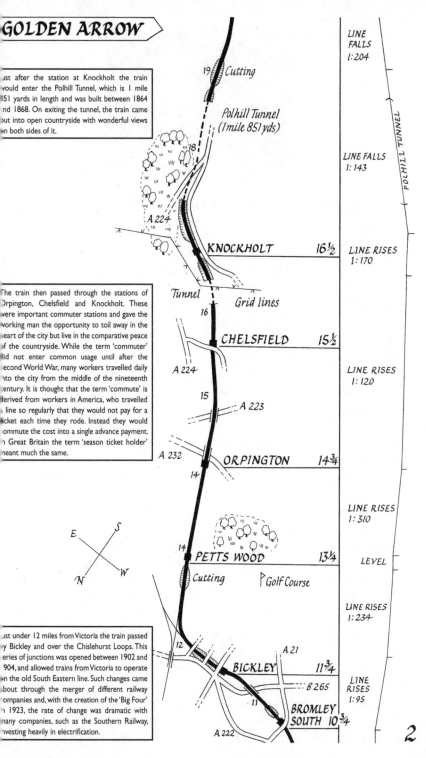

GOLDEN ARROW

Just after the station at Knockholt the train would enter the Polhill Tunnel, which is 1 mile 851 yards in length and was built between 1864 and 1868. On exiting the tunnel, the train came out into open countryside with wonderful views on both sides of it.

The train then passed through the stations of Orpington, Chelsfield and Knockholt. These were important commuter stations and gave the working man the opportunity to toil away in the heart of the city but live in the comparative peace of the countryside. While the term 'commuter' did not enter common usage until after the Second World War, many workers travelled daily into the city from the middle of the nineteenth century. It is thought that the term 'commute' is derived from workers in America, who travelled a line so regularly that they would not pay for a ticket each time they rode. Instead they would commute the cost into a single advance payment. In Great Britain the term 'season ticket holder' meant much the same.

Just under 12 miles from Victoria the train passed by Bickley and over the Chislehurst Loops. This series of junctions was opened between 1902 and 1904, and allowed trains from Victoria to operate on the old South Eastern line. Such changes came about through the merger of different railway companies and, with the creation of the 'Big Four' in 1923, the rate of change was dramatic with many companies, such as the Southern Railway, investing heavily in electrification.

19 Cutting

Polhill Tunnel
(1 mile 851 yds)

18

A 224

KNOCKHOLT   16½

Tunnel   16
Grid lines

CHELSFIELD   15½

A 224

15   A 223

A 232   ORPINGTON   14¾
14

14   PETTS WOOD   13¼
Cutting   Golf Course

12
BICKLEY   11¾   A 21
B 265
11
BROMLEY
SOUTH 10¾
A 222

LINE
FALLS
1:204

POLHILL TUNNEL

LINE FALLS
1:143

LINE RISES
1:170

LINE RISES
1:120

LINE RISES
1:310

LEVEL

LINE RISES
1:234

LINE
RISES
1:95

E   S

N   W

2

13

London in the Nineteenth Century

The railways had an impact on almost all aspects of society in the nineteenth century. They transformed agriculture, trade and industry, and they changed the towns and cities that they connected. Some towns, like Swindon and Crewe, are truly railway towns. Their entire existence is due to the fact that railway companies based their locomotive works at strategic points along the line and then built houses for the workers that they employed. Schools, churches and shops were all built for the workers and busy towns sprang up that had a look and feel all of their own.

London, however, was already a huge bustling metropolis before the arrival of the railways but, by the 1830s, railways and railway architecture were beginning to make their mark on the face of the capital. Euston station was opened in 1837 and was followed by King's Cross in 1852 and the main Paddington station in 1854. The pace of building increased through the century and there were another seven terminals opened in London between 1860 and 1875. The building of the railways themselves, the viaducts and the grand stations

in London led to many labourers, or navigators, moving into the city.

But it was not just an influx of cheap labour that helped to change the face of London in the railway age. Railways allowed people to live near the city and travel to and from work each day, and from as early as the mid-1840s, the commuter began to appear. Commuters were originally those who held season tickets to travel on the railway and, instead of paying a daily fare, 'commuted' it into a single instalment. Records of ticket sales show that by the 1850s, the number of people travelling in this way was on the increase.

At around the same time the railway companies, quick to spot a business opportunity, began to encourage speculative building alongside their lines into the city on the premise that if more people lived alongside their lines, then more of them would use their trains to get to and from work each day. Very often, once the houses were built the railway companies would provide cheap season tickets for a limited time to encourage people to move in.

By the 1860s the railways were

putting on special Workmen's Trains, which provided cheap transport for workers into the city. These left early in the morning and returned in the evening, and allowed even more people to live outside of the city centre in areas that, while perhaps once separate from the city, were now becoming suburbs as they rapidly expanded.

In 1801, the population of London was put at 958,863 but by 1899, it had grown by more than five times to 6,528,434. Many new jobs and opportunities came about because of the Industrial Revolution and there was a general shift from a rural population to an urban one. Without the railways such a shift would not have been possible. Not only did they provide the means of transport allowing people to get to work each day but they were also closely involved in the building of suburbs that helped the city to expand. The Eurostar – like the Golden Arrow before it – moves through a city that has been fundamentally shaped and re-formed by the railways.

Opposite: London sandwich men resting in the Strand, 1884
Above: Looking west across the Thames, 1845

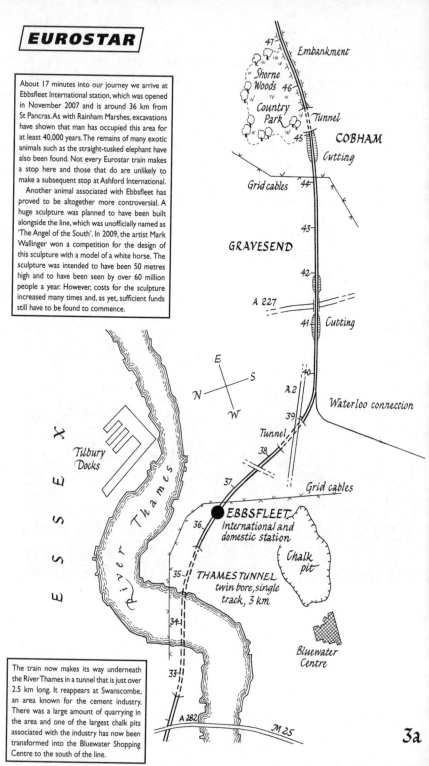

EUROSTAR

About 17 minutes into our journey we arrive at Ebbsfleet International station, which was opened in November 2007 and is around 36 km from St Pancras. As with Rainham Marshes, excavations have shown that man has occupied this area for at least 40,000 years. The remains of many exotic animals such as the straight-tusked elephant have also been found. Not every Eurostar train makes a stop here and those that do are unlikely to make a subsequent stop at Ashford International.

Another animal associated with Ebbsfleet has proved to be altogether more controversial. A huge sculpture was planned to have been built alongside the line, which was unofficially named as 'The Angel of the South'. In 2009, the artist Mark Wallinger won a competition for the design of this sculpture with a model of a white horse. The sculpture was intended to have been 50 metres high and to have been seen by over 60 million people a year. However, costs for the sculpture increased many times and, as yet, sufficient funds still have to be found to commence.

The train now makes its way underneath the River Thames in a tunnel that is just over 2.5 km long. It reappears at Swanscombe, an area known for the cement industry. There was a large amount of quarrying in the area and one of the largest chalk pits associated with the industry has now been transformed into the Bluewater Shopping Centre to the south of the line.

Embankment
Shorne Woods Country Park
47
46
45 Tunnel
COBHAM
Cutting
Grid cables
44
43
GRAVESEND
42
A 227
41 Cutting
40
A 2
Waterloo connection
39
Tunnel
38
37
Grid cables
EBBSFLEET International and domestic station
36
Chalk pit
35 THAMES TUNNEL twin bore, single track, 3 km
34
Bluewater Centre
33
A 282
M 25

ESSEX
Tilbury Docks
River Thames

E
S
N
W

3a

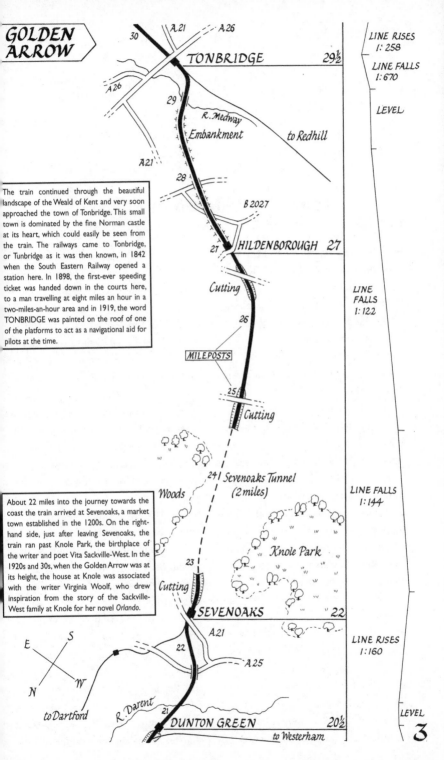

GOLDEN ARROW

A 21   A 26
30
TONBRIDGE   29½

A 26
29
R. Medway
Embankment   to Redhill

A 21
28

B 2027

27   **HILDENBOROUGH** 27

Cutting

26

MILE POSTS

25
Cutting

24
Sevenoaks Tunnel
(2 miles)

Woods

23
Cutting

SEVENOAKS   22

22
A 21

A 25

E   S
N   W

to Dartford

R. Darent
21
DUNTON GREEN   20½
to Westerham

LINE RISES
1: 258

LINE FALLS
1: 670

LEVEL

LINE FALLS
1: 122

LINE FALLS
1: 144

LINE RISES
1: 160

LEVEL

3

Knole Park

The train continued through the beautiful landscape of the Weald of Kent and very soon approached the town of Tonbridge. This small town is dominated by the fine Norman castle at its heart, which could easily be seen from the train. The railways came to Tonbridge, or Tunbridge as it was then known, in 1842 when the South Eastern Railway opened a station here. In 1898, the first-ever speeding ticket was handed down in the courts here, to a man travelling at eight miles an hour in a two-miles-an-hour area and in 1919, the word TONBRIDGE was painted on the roof of one of the platforms to act as a navigational aid for pilots at the time.

About 22 miles into the journey towards the coast the train arrived at Sevenoaks, a market town established in the 1200s. On the right-hand side, just after leaving Sevenoaks, the train ran past Knole Park, the birthplace of the writer and poet Vita Sackville-West. In the 1920s and 30s, when the Golden Arrow was at its height, the house at Knole was associated with the writer Virginia Woolf, who drew inspiration from the story of the Sackville-West family at Knole for her novel *Orlando*.

Kent: The Garden of England

Both the Eurostar and the Golden Arrow pass through the county of Kent on their way to the coast. For many years Kent has been known as 'The Garden of England' due to the abundance of orchards and hop-gardens, and the quantity and quality of the crops. The landscape of the county has been formed through the weathering of successive layers of greensand, sandstone and chalk, which has created the undulating topography of the North and South Downs, with the lower Weald running between the two. The chalk geology of eastern Kent is remarkably similar to that of wine-producing areas of France and, in recent years, several award-winning wines have been produced from the vineyards that have been established in the area.

However, it is for orchards and hop-gardens that Kent is perhaps most famous. Sadly, since the Second World War, Kent has lost around 85 per cent of its orchards, mainly due to changes in agricultural practices and the development of land. Cherry, pear and apple orchards that were established centuries ago have been grubbed up

in the last 60 years. There are many varieties of eating and cooking apple from the county, which, although rare, have been preserved, such as *Bascombe's Mystery* and *Mabbott's Pearmain*. Unlike in the West Country, the local cider is usually produced from a mix of eating and cooking varieties as opposed to specific cider apples.

Kent's hop-gardens have been famous since the nineteenth century, when the tradition developed for families from the East End of London to take holidays in the Kent countryside and work as casual labour to harvest the hops. However, hops have been grown in Kent since the 1500s. The hops were a vital ingredient in the brewing industry, not only adding flavour but also acting as a preservative. Before the widespread availability of clean drinking water, weak, or small, beer was the everyday drink of choice throughout much of the country and Kentish hops were in great demand. Hops are incredibly quick-growing and the hop-gardens were created by erecting a series of poles that were held upright with a complex arrangement of wires. The hop 'bines' grew up the

KENT - THE GARDEN OF ENGLAND

SEE BRITAIN BY TRAIN

poles and along the wires before being harvested by hand.

When travelling through the Kent countryside some of the most easily recognisable buildings that can be seen from the train are the oast houses attached to almost every farm. There are descriptions of them dating back as far as the 1570s, but in the main, they date from the nineteenth century. These tall, often conical, structures have tiled roofs surmounted by a characteristic cowl. They were used for drying out the hops and consist of a series of thin perforated floors on which the hops were spread out. A small fire was lit in a kiln at the bottom of the building and the cowl turned to the wind to allow the heat to escape. Although the number of hop-gardens in the county has shrunk dramatically, the oast houses have remained in the landscape as a testament to the county's agricultural past. While a small number of oast houses are still in use today, many of them have been converted into private homes.

Above: A poster produced for British Railways to promote rail service in Kent, 1955

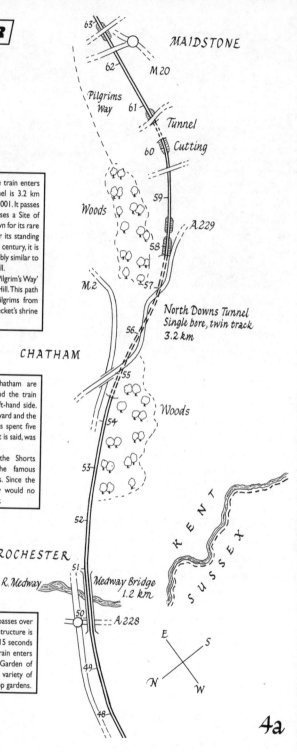

Around 56 km from St Pancras the train enters the North Down Tunnel. The tunnel is 3.2 km long and was opened in December 2001. It passes under Blue Bell Hill, which comprises a Site of Special Scientific Interest (SSSI) known for its rare plant species. This area is known for its standing stones and, until the early twentieth century, it is known that a stone monument, possibly similar to the nearby *Kit's Coty*, stood on the hill.

The ancient track known as the 'Pilgrim's Way' runs along the bottom of Blue Bell Hill. This path is reputedly the route taken by pilgrims from Hampshire in the West to Thomas Becket's shrine at Canterbury in the East.

The towns of Rochester and Chatham are situated either side of the river and the train passes close by Chatham on the left-hand side. Chatham is famous for its naval dockyard and the fact that the author Charles Dickens spent five years here as a child – a time which, it is said, was to prove influential on his writing.

Rochester was the home of the Shorts aeroplane factory which built the famous Sunderland and 'Empire' flying boats. Since the building of the Medway bridge they would no longer be able to take off up the river.

On leaving Ebbsfleet the train quickly passes over the Medway Viaduct. This impressive structure is 1.2 km long and it takes only around 15 seconds to cross. Once over the bridge the train enters the county of Kent, known as 'The Garden of England' because of the quantity and variety of produce grown in the orchards and hop gardens.

4a

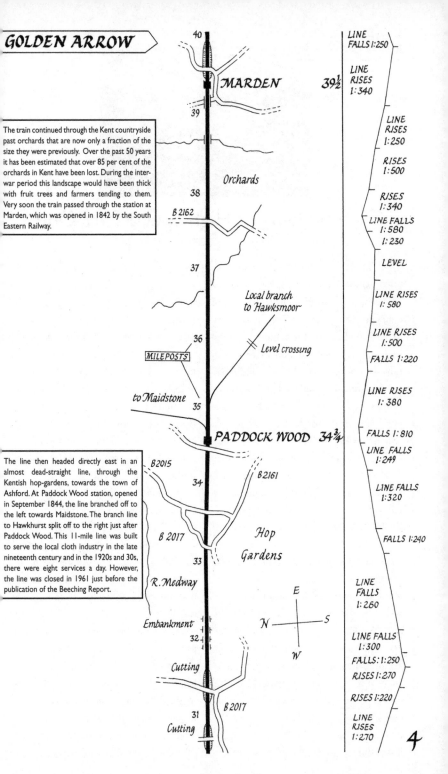

GOLDEN ARROW

40

MARDEN

39

39½

The train continued through the Kent countryside past orchards that are now only a fraction of the size they were previously. Over the past 50 years it has been estimated that over 85 per cent of the orchards in Kent have been lost. During the inter-war period this landscape would have been thick with fruit trees and farmers tending to them. Very soon the train passed through the station at Marden, which was opened in 1842 by the South Eastern Railway.

LINE
FALLS 1:250

LINE
RISES
1:340

LINE
RISES
1:250

RISES
1:500

RISES
1:340

LINE FALLS
1:580

1:230

LEVEL

Orchards

38

B 2162

37

Local branch
to Hawksmoor

Level crossing

36

MILEPOSTS

to Maidstone

35

LINE RISES
1:580

LINE RISES
1:500

FALLS 1:220

LINE RISES
1:380

PADDOCK WOOD 34¾

FALLS 1:810

LINE FALLS
1:249

B 2015

The line then headed directly east in an almost dead-straight line, through the Kentish hop-gardens, towards the town of Ashford. At Paddock Wood station, opened in September 1844, the line branched off to the left towards Maidstone. The branch line to Hawkhurst split off to the right just after Paddock Wood. This 11-mile line was built to serve the local cloth industry in the late nineteenth century and in the 1920s and 30s, there were eight services a day. However, the line was closed in 1961 just before the publication of the Beeching Report.

B 2161

34

Hop
Gardens

B 2017

33

R. Medway

LINE FALLS
1:320

FALLS 1:240

E

N   S

W

LINE
FALLS
1:260

Embankment

32

LINE FALLS
1:300

FALLS: 1:250

RISES 1:270

Cutting

RISES 1:220

31

B 2017

Cutting

LINE
RISES
1:270

4

21

The Building of High Speed, Part One

The Channel Tunnel Rail Link, or High Speed 1 (HS1) as it has come to be known, is the 67-mile railway that connects St Pancras station in London to the British side of the Channel Tunnel in Kent. The construction of any new railway line is an enormous challenge and building one that would allow trains to travel at speeds of up to 186 miles per hour was particularly complex. Altogether the project cost £5.8 billion and it was tackled in two sections. Section 1 ran from the tunnel portal just outside Dover to Fawkham Junction in north Kent; Section 2 completed the line from Kent into St Pancras station.

Section 1 was begun in October 1998 and opened in September 2003. Once opened, the journey time between Waterloo station (the Eurostar terminal while St Pancras was being rebuilt) and the Channel Tunnel was cut by 20 minutes. This section was some 46 miles long and along its length were some of the engineering triumphs of the entire project. The Medway Viaduct in particular was singled out for praise for its elegance and simplicity. When built, it was the longest high-speed rail bridge

in the world and provided a 'cruelly short', but spectacular, 15-second view down the Medway Valley. The North Downs Tunnel was also a remarkable piece of engineering. It is just under two miles in length and runs 100 metres beneath Blue Bell Hill, a Site of Special Scientific Interest and the location of several important archaeological sites. Amazingly, the work was organised so well that the tunnel was completed six months early and £5 million under budget.

Section 2 is 24.5 miles in length, was begun in 2001 and opened in November 2007. This saw the line brought through East London and into the newly rebuilt St Pancras station, along with the construction of stations at Ebbsfleet and Stratford. Ebbsfleet International, due to its proximity to the A2/M2 trunk road, has been dubbed 'the ultimate park and ride' and, at 50 hectares, was the largest area of development on the Channel Tunnel project after St Pancras itself. When designed and constructed, it was estimated that the station would have a catchment area of more than 10 million people. After this section of

HS1 was opened, it cut another 20 minutes off the journey time to Paris, making the French capital just 2 hours and 15 minutes away from London.

There are high-speed rail networks in several other countries, such as France and Germany. Perhaps the most famous, and certainly the first, is the Shinkansen in Japan, which opened in time for the Japanese Olympics in 1964. The railway network in Great Britain is still very much a product of its Victorian origins, which limits its ability to grow and change, and issues of conservation rightly constrain development. This makes the achievement of HS1 all the more remarkable. That the line has proved to be a success is shown by the fact that, in 2010 alone, 9.5 million passengers used the service to travel between Great Britain and the capitals of Europe.

Opposite: The Eurostar crossing the Medway Viaduct en route to St Pancras, 2003
Above: The Eurostar travels towards the Channel Tunnel in Kent, 2010

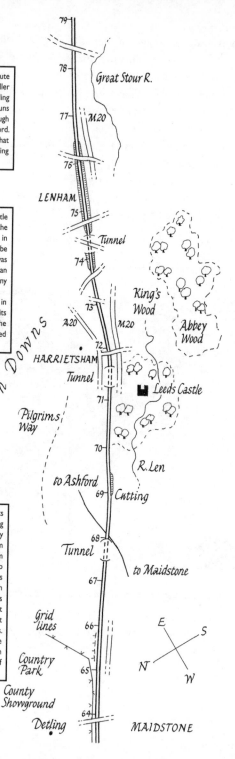

For several kilometres the train follows the route of the Great Stour River which, while smaller than the Medway, was an important trading route for the county of Kent. The river runs to the right of the train and meanders through the countryside towards the town of Ashford. Along its length were numerous water mills that provided power for industries such as grinding corn and paper-making.

Only about 5 km past Maidstone, Leeds Castle comes into view on the right-hand side of the train. The castle is built entirely on islands in the middle of a lake and is considered to be among the most beautiful in the country. It was originally constructed in 1119 by a Norman knight but has been added to and rebuilt many times over its almost 900 years of history.

The castle was extensively remodelled in the early nineteenth century and much of its appearance dates from this period. In 2004, the castle hosted the Northern Irish peace talks led by the then Prime Minister Tony Blair.

Maidstone is the county town of Kent and its name may refer to a now-disappeared standing stone, of which there were many in the Medway Valley. Much of the town's wealth came from river trade, which allowed the produce from the fertile farmland to be sold and shipped to London, only 50 km downriver. As the train leaves Maidstone it makes its way through the North Downs and to the left of the track, the Pilgrims Way continues onward to Canterbury. About 4 km along we enter the first of several short tunnels that take the train through the Downs. These tunnels were constructed to minimise the environmental impact of High Speed 1 on the chalk hills that are considered to be Areas of Outstanding Natural Beauty.

5a

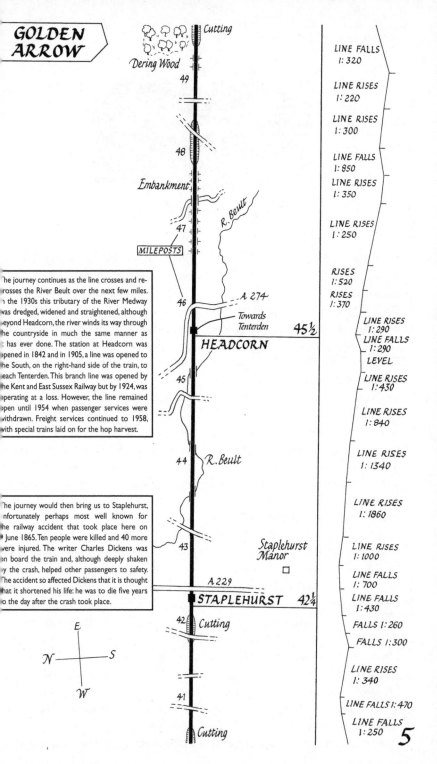

GOLDEN
ARROW

Cutting

Dering Wood

49

48

Embankment

R. Beult

47

MILEPOSTS

The journey continues as the line crosses and re-crosses the River Beult over the next few miles. In the 1930s this tributary of the River Medway was dredged, widened and straightened, although beyond Headcorn, the river winds its way through the countryside in much the same manner as it has ever done. The station at Headcorn was opened in 1842 and in 1905, a line was opened to the South, on the right-hand side of the train, to reach Tenterden. This branch line was opened by the Kent and East Sussex Railway but by 1924, was operating at a loss. However, the line remained open until 1954 when passenger services were withdrawn. Freight services continued to 1958, with special trains laid on for the hop harvest.

46

A 274

Towards
Tenterden

45½

HEADCORN

45

44   R. Beult

The journey would then bring us to Staplehurst, unfortunately perhaps most well known for the railway accident that took place here on 9 June 1865. Ten people were killed and 40 more were injured. The writer Charles Dickens was on board the train and, although deeply shaken by the crash, helped other passengers to safety. The accident so affected Dickens that it is thought that it shortened his life: he was to die five years to the day after the crash took place.

43

Staplehurst
Manor

☐

A 229

STAPLEHURST   42¼

42 Cutting

E

N ——————— S

W

41

Cutting

LINE FALLS
1:320

LINE RISES
1:220

LINE RISES
1:300

LINE FALLS
1:850

LINE RISES
1:350

LINE RISES
1:250

RISES
1:520

RISES
1:370

LINE RISES
1:290

LINE FALLS
1:290

LEVEL

LINE RISES
1:430

LINE RISES
1:840

LINE RISES
1:1340

LINE RISES
1:1860

LINE RISES
1:1000

LINE FALLS
1:700

LINE FALLS
1:430

FALLS 1:260

FALLS 1:300

LINE RISES
1:340

LINE FALLS 1:470

LINE FALLS
1:250

5

25

The Golden Arrow

Until the opening of the Channel Tunnel, all of Great Britain's railways ended, unsurprisingly, at the coast. But this has never stopped railway companies from thinking about how to get passengers over the Channel. Continental travel has always had an appeal and the railways were quick to get in on the act and tap into another potential market.

From the earliest days of railway travel, railway companies had designs on the continent. Among the first to make serious inroads into providing a cross-Channel service was the South Eastern Railway (SER). In 1843, the SER bought the harbour at Folkestone from the Government and made it their primary port for steam packet services to Calais and Boulogne. But, as a railway company, they had no powers to run a shipping organisation, so they set up a subsidiary company called the South Eastern & Continental Steam Packet Company. The SER were quickly followed by the London, Chatham and Dover Railway (LCDR) – whose line to Dover, opened in 1861, almost two decades after the SER's own station in

Dover – meant that they too could begin operating cross-Channel services.

The rivalry between the two railway companies would continue throughout the remainder of the nineteenth century and in 1889 both companies announced the introduction of new, entirely first-class, services from London to the continent within weeks of each other. This was the year of the Great Exhibition in Paris with the (now iconic) Eiffel Tower and more people than ever wanted to make the crossing and visit France. In the end the two railway companies decided to work together with their French counterparts and the Club Train, the precursor to the Golden Arrow, was born. However, low ticket sales in the 1890s meant that the service only survived until September 1893.

It was not until 1923 that another serious attempt was made to set up a first-class deluxe service from London to the continent. The amalgamation of the railway companies into the Big Four meant that the administration of such a service would be considerably easier, as the Southern Railway (SR) would be

he only company involved on this side
of the Channel.

The service was to be called the
Golden Arrow, named after the French
service from Calais to Paris, La Flèche
D'or, and the SR commissioned a new
steamship, the SS *Canterbury*, which
would be dedicated to the service.
Only those who had a Golden Arrow
ticket would be allowed on board, thus
significantly reducing crowding and
increasing the comfort of those who had
paid the £5 single fare from Victoria in
London to Paris Gare du Nord.

From 1931-35, almost 3,500,000
railway passengers crossed the Channel,
although not all of them would have
been able to afford the high cost of

a ticket on the Golden Arrow. The
journey time from London to Paris was
just over five-and-a-half hours and the
Pullman carriages used on the trip
made life exceptionally comfortable for
the passengers.

The service continued until the
outbreak of the Second World War
and then recommenced in April 1946
although by this time there were a certain
number of second-class carriages in
the train formation. While there were
changes to the service, the Golden
Arrow continued until September 1972
and it has been argued that, not until
the introduction of the Eurostar, with its
mix of speed and comfort, was the same
level of luxury achieved again.

Opposite: The Golden Arrow Pullman train from Victoria to Dover,
at Stewarts Lane Depot, Battersea
Above: Even in the austere 1940s Pullman cars exuded an alluring opulence

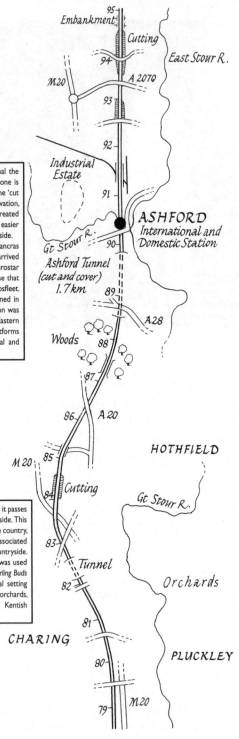

95
Embankment
Cutting
East Stour R.
94
M20
A 2070
93
92
Industrial
Estate
91
ASHFORD
International and
Domestic Station
Gt Stour R.
90
Ashford Tunnel
(cut and cover)
1.7 km
89
A 28
Woods
88
87
86
A 20
HOTHFIELD
85
M 20
Gt Stour R.
84
Cutting
83
Tunnel
82
Orchards
81
CHARING
80
PLUCKLEY
79
M 20

Just before arriving in Ashford International the train passes through another tunnel. This one is 1.7 km long and was constructed using the 'cut and cover' method where a large excavation, or cut, is first made and the tunnel created by being covered over. This is often an easier method than boring a tunnel through a hillside.

Ashford International is 90 km from St Pancras and, all being well, the train will have arrived here in around 32 minutes. Not every Eurostar train makes a stop at this station and those that do have not stopped previously at Ebbsfleet. The rebuilt international station was opened in February 1996, although the original station was opened in December 1842 by the South Eastern Railway. The station has a total of six platforms and handles over 2.7 million international and domestic passengers each year.

As the train makes its way towards Ashford it passes the village of Pluckley on the right-hand side. This village claims to be the most haunted in the country, with a long list of ghosts and spectres associated with the buildings and surrounding countryside. Whatever its otherworldly credentials, it was used for the setting of the drama series *The Darling Buds of May* where it stood in for the original setting of Sidcup. The village is surrounded by orchards, where local apples such as Falstaff or Kentish Filbasket would have been grown.

E
S
N
W

6

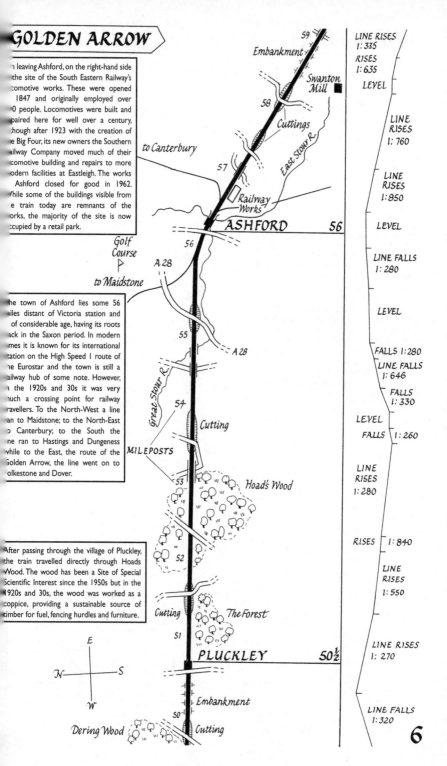

GOLDEN ARROW

n leaving Ashford, on the right-hand side
the site of the South Eastern Railway's
comotive works. These were opened
1847 and originally employed over
0 people. Locomotives were built and
paired here for well over a century,
hough after 1923 with the creation of
e Big Four, its new owners the Southern
ailway Company moved much of their
comotive building and repairs to more
odern facilities at Eastleigh. The works
Ashford closed for good in 1962.
While some of the buildings visible from
e train today are remnants of the
orks, the majority of the site is now
ccupied by a retail park.

he town of Ashford lies some 56
iles distant of Victoria station and
of considerable age, having its roots
ack in the Saxon period. In modern
mes it is known for its international
tation on the High Speed 1 route of
e Eurostar and the town is still a
ailway hub of some note. However,
n the 1920s and 30s it was very
uch a crossing point for railway
ravellers. To the North-West a line
an to Maidstone; to the North-East
Canterbury; to the South the
ne ran to Hastings and Dungeness
while to the East, the route of the
Golden Arrow, the line went on to
olkestone and Dover.

After passing through the village of Pluckley,
the train travelled directly through Hoads
Wood. The wood has been a Site of Special
Scientific Interest since the 1950s but in the
1920s and 30s, the wood was worked as a
coppice, providing a sustainable source of
timber for fuel, fencing hurdles and furniture.

Embankment
59

Swanton Mill

58

Cuttings

East Stour R.

to Canterbury

57

Railway Works

ASHFORD   56

Golf Course

56

A 28

to Maidstone

55

A 28

Great Stour R.

54

Cutting

MILEPOSTS

53   Hoad's Wood

52

Cutting   The Forest

51

PLUCKLEY   50½

E
N — S
W

Dering Wood   50   Cutting

Embankment

LINE RISES
1: 335
RISES
1: 635
LEVEL

LINE RISES
1: 760

LINE RISES
1: 850

LEVEL

LINE FALLS
1: 280

LEVEL

FALLS 1: 280
LINE FALLS
1: 646
FALLS
1: 330
LEVEL
FALLS   1: 260

LINE RISES
1: 280

RISES   1: 840

LINE RISES
1: 550

LINE RISES
1: 270

LINE FALLS
1: 320

6

29

EUROSTAR

110

FOLKESTONE DISTRICT

English Channel

M 20

109

Pilgrims Way

108

Royal Military Canal

Asholt Wood

107

A 20

106

HYTHE

105 *Tunnel*

Only a few minutes after leaving Ashford the train passes by the village of Westenhanger and from the right-hand side, Westenhanger Castle can be seen, side by side with the grandstand of Folkestone racecourse.

The castle was originally a manor house that dated back to Saxon times but it was fortified in the fourteenth century although, as with Leeds Castle, the buildings have been much altered over the years. Folkestone Racecourse was first opened in the late nineteenth century and, along with horse racing, has had a close association with aviation. From 1910, aircraft have landed on the course and during the Second World War, it was entirely given over to the RAF.

104

B 2068

WESTENHANGER

103

Castle

Folkestone Racecourse

102

Embankment

A 20

101

SELINDGE

Grid lines

E
N —— S
W

100

Grid lines *Cutting*

99

BRABOURNE LEES

98

Deer Park

97

Cutting

96

R. Stour

MERSHAM

Manor Ho.

95

Tunnel

Orchards

On leaving Ashford the train continues through the Kent countryside, passing by the villages of Mersham and Brabourne Lees on the left-hand side. The village of Mersham has been the home of the Knatchbull family since the sixteenth century and the village church of St John the Baptist may just be seen as the train travels past.

Just to the north of Mersham is Hatch Park, a Site of Special Scientific Interest that is the remains of an ancient deer park. The park contains pollarded trees, an example of a wildlife habitat not usually found in this part of the country. It is thought that the ground in the park has not been put to the plough for over 500 years.

7a

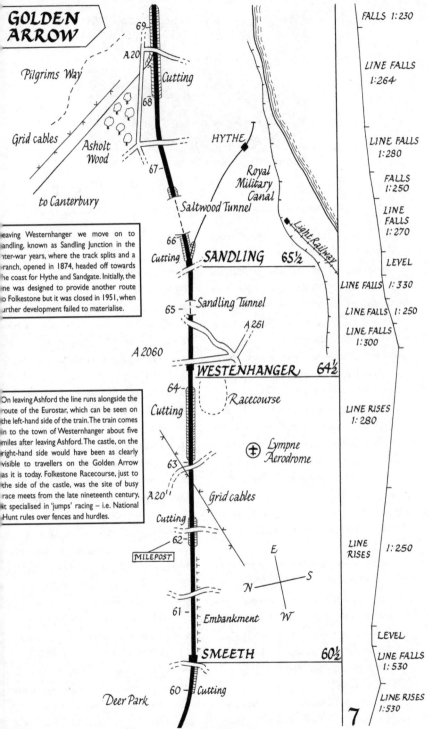

GOLDEN ARROW

Pilgrims Way

Grid cables

Asholt Wood

to Canterbury

A20

69

68

67

Cutting

HYTHE

Royal Military Canal

Saltwood Tunnel

Light Railway

66

Cutting

SANDLING   65½

65

Sandling Tunnel

A 261

A 2060

WESTENHANGER   64½

64

Cutting

Racecourse

63

⊕ Lympne Aerodrome

A 20

Grid cables

Cutting

62

MILEPOST

E

S

N

W

61

Embankment

SMEETH   60½

60

Cutting

Deer Park

FALLS 1:230

LINE FALLS 1:264

LINE FALLS 1:280

FALLS 1:250

LINE FALLS 1:270

LEVEL

LINE FALLS 1:330

LINE FALLS 1:250

LINE FALLS 1:300

LINE RISES 1:280

LINE RISES 1:250

LEVEL

LINE FALLS 1:530

LINE RISES 1:530

7

eaving Westernhanger we move on to andling, known as Sandling Junction in the nter-war years, where the track splits and a branch, opened in 1874, headed off towards he coast for Hythe and Sandgate. Initially, the ne was designed to provide another route o Folkestone but it was closed in 1951, when urther development failed to materialise.

On leaving Ashford the line runs alongside the route of the Eurostar, which can be seen on the left-hand side of the train. The train comes in to the town of Westernhanger about five miles after leaving Ashford. The castle, on the right-hand side would have been as clearly visible to travellers on the Golden Arrow as it is today. Folkestone Racecourse, just to the side of the castle, was the site of busy race meets from the late nineteenth century, it specialised in 'jumps' racing – i.e. National Hunt rules over fences and hurdles.

The Eurostar Reaches the Coast

The Channel Tunnel Rail Link (CTRL), or HS1 as it is more commonly known, passes through some of the most beautiful and archaeologically rich landscapes in England. During the construction of the line millions of pounds were spent carrying out archaeological excavations along the route and care was taken to ensure that there was minimal impact on wildlife wherever possible.

The excavations began in the late 1990s and, taken as a whole, the work on High Speed I constituted the largest archaeological project ever undertaken in the United Kingdom. There were more than 100 specialists working on the project and, at the beginning of the work, they outnumbered the construction workers on the site.

Finds from every period of Britain's history were uncovered in the work. From prehistoric landscapes where man coexisted with mammoths to the Second World War remains, almost every part of the route of High Speed 1 revealed a snapshot of what everyday life was like in the past.

But the discoveries were not just underground. Several ancient buildings were either completely dismantled or were moved whole as they were too close to the proposed line. Bridge House, in the village of Mersham, was one such building. It took six months of preparation but, over the course of two days, the entire building, which dated back to the sixteenth century, was moved 50 metres uphill away from the railway cutting. It took only 10 people to achieve this although over one tonne of grease was used to slide the building along. The farmhouse at Brockton, rather than being dismantled and moved to the Weald and Downland Museum at Singleton. While this was taking place a curious deposit was found sealed within one of the walls. It contained shoes, gloves and three mummified cats. The tradition of placing objects around and within buildings to ward off bad luck goes back thousands of years but this was much more recent, dating perhaps to the eighteenth or nineteenth centuries.

High Speed 1 also ran through a number of Sites of Special Scientific Interest (or SSSIs) and care was taken to minimise the impact of the work on the plants and animals in these areas

Blue Bell Hill is one such example. Many of the tunnels along the route of High Speed 1 ensure that the Eurostar travels underneath such sensitive sites and causes as little damage as possible.

It should be remembered that the archaeological work was not limited to the English side of the route. There are ongoing issues in northern France relating to finds of unexploded artillery shells from both the World Wars. These make life extremely difficult, and dangerous, for the local farmers. French engineers also encountered these problems when the TGV lines were constructed. While not archaeology in the more common sense of the word, they are nonetheless reminders of past events in the landscape and a lasting testament to the battles that were fought there.

Other problems, of a more unexpected nature, were encountered once the line was actually constructed. Perhaps most famous was the refugee camp at the town of Sangatte. Asylum seekers gathered here to attempt the crossing into the UK on both freight and passenger services, and the Red Cross, responding to the need to provide basic facilities, set up a camp in 1999. Refugees from the Middle East, Africa and Eastern Europe made their way to Sangatte (later nicknamed 'Sans-Gate' or 'without gates') in an attempt to find a better life.

Many were injured and several refugees died while trying to stow away and there were riots when attempts were made to close the camp down. Relations between France and England became increasingly strained and eventually the camp was closed in 2002. Many millions of pounds were also spent on additional security and CCTV cameras. While there are still attempts made to gain access to the UK on the Eurostar, the numbers of people attempting this have dropped from around 250 a week to only a handful. It is a reminder that the railways are not only a convenient way to get to a business meeting or to go on holiday. For some they can be a last resort in the attempt to find something safer or more rewarding, and some pay for their journey with their lives.

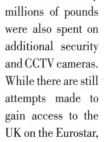

Opposite: The Golden Arrow at the White Cliffs of Dover, 1946, usually hauled by one of Southern Railway's Lord Nelson class locomotives
Above: French SNCF railway police patrol a freight terminal near Sangatte

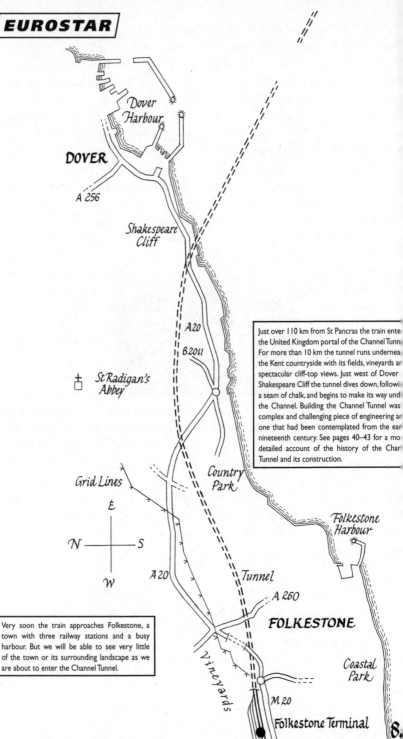

Dover Harbour

DOVER

A 256

Shakespeare Cliff

A 20

B 2011

✝ St Radigan's Abbey

Grid Lines

E

N —— S

W

A 20

Country Park

Just over 110 km from St Pancras the train ente
the United Kingdom portal of the Channel Tunn
For more than 10 km the tunnel runs undernea
the Kent countryside with its fields, vineyards ar
spectacular cliff-top views. Just west of Dover
Shakespeare Cliff the tunnel dives down, followi
a seam of chalk, and begins to make its way und
the Channel. Building the Channel Tunnel was
complex and challenging piece of engineering ar
one that had been contemplated from the ear
nineteenth century. See pages 40–43 for a mo
detailed account of the history of the Char
Tunnel and its construction.

Folkestone Harbour

Tunnel

A 260

FOLKESTONE

Coastal Park

Very soon the train approaches Folkestone, a
town with three railway stations and a busy
harbour. But we will be able to see very little
of the town or its surrounding landscape as we
are about to enter the Channel Tunnel.

Vineyards

M 20

Folkestone Terminal

8.

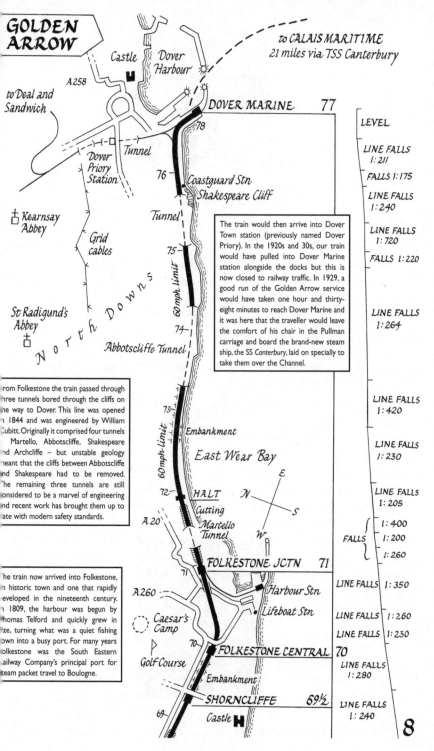

GOLDEN ARROW

to CALAIS MARITIME
21 miles via TSS Canterbury

Castle   Dover Harbour

A258

to Deal and Sandwich

DOVER MARINE   77

78

Dover Priory Station

Tunnel

✝ Kearnsay Abbey

Grid cables

76 — Coastguard Stn
Shakespeare Cliff

Tunnel

75

St Radigund's Abbey ✝

North Downs

74

Abbotscliffe Tunnel

60mph limit

The train would then arrive into Dover Town station (previously named Dover Priory). In the 1920s and 30s, our train would have pulled into Dover Marine station alongside the docks but this is now closed to railway traffic. In 1929, a good run of the Golden Arrow service would have taken one hour and thirty-eight minutes to reach Dover Marine and it was here that the traveller would leave the comfort of his chair in the Pullman carriage and board the brand-new steam ship, the SS *Canterbury*, laid on specially to take them over the Channel.

73

Embankment

East Wear Bay

E
N
S
W

60mph limit

72 — HALT
Cutting

A20

Martello Tunnel

FOLKESTONE JCTN   71

71

A260

Caesar's Camp

Harbour Stn
Lifeboat Stn

70

Golf Course

FOLKESTONE CENTRAL   70

Embankment

SHORNCLIFFE   69½

69

Castle ⌘

From Folkestone the train passed through three tunnels bored through the cliffs on the way to Dover. This line was opened in 1844 and was engineered by William Cubitt. Originally it comprised four tunnels — Martello, Abbotscliffe, Shakespeare and Archcliffe — but unstable geology meant that the cliffs between Abbotscliffe and Shakespeare had to be removed. The remaining three tunnels are still considered to be a marvel of engineering and recent work has brought them up to date with modern safety standards.

The train now arrived into Folkestone, an historic town and one that rapidly developed in the nineteenth century. In 1809, the harbour was begun by Thomas Telford and quickly grew in size, turning what was a quiet fishing town into a busy port. For many years Folkestone was the South Eastern Railway Company's principal port for steam packet travel to Boulogne.

LEVEL

LINE FALLS 1:211

FALLS 1:175

LINE FALLS 1:240

LINE FALLS 1:720

FALLS 1:220

LINE FALLS 1:264

LINE FALLS 1:420

LINE FALLS 1:230

LINE FALLS 1:205

1:400
FALLS   1:200
1:260

LINE FALLS 1:350

LINE FALLS 1:260

LINE FALLS 1:230

LINE FALLS 1:280

LINE FALLS 1:240

8

Crossing the Channel

A first-class single fare on the Golden Arrow cost five pounds in 1929 and this covered not only the railway journeys from Victoria to Dover and Calais to Paris but also the crossing of the Channel. While the Southern Railway had a number of vessels for channel crossings it was the SS *Canterbury*, built by Messrs. William Denny and Brothers of Dumbarton, that was to become the flagship for the service.

Passengers disembarked from the train and made their way to the ship on foot, with porters carrying their luggage. Arrangements were made to ensure that any customs inspections were as quick and convenient as possible. Interestingly, items such as firearms, opium, heroin, cocaine and hashish were not banned. One simply needed to pay the correct duty on them!

When first launched in 1929, the *Canterbury* was for the exclusive use of the Golden Arrow passengers. It was designed to be the smoothest crossing possible and allowed

them to make the one-and-a-quarter hour journey in comfort and luxury. One passenger, travelling in June 1929, has this to say about the Channel crossing on board the *Canterbury*:

'Her promenade deck is one long arm-chaired winter garden. When not chatting there, we are in her Garden Café astern; or in the oak panelled smoking-room; or at the buffet; or in the Parisian-looking restaurant. And there is no semblance of a crowd.'

However, the Great Depression soon put an end to this exclusivity and, as the Golden Arrow itself was retimed, the *Canterbury*'s sailings were moved forward to allow passengers from the ordinary train to board her. By 1932, she was also taking the second-class passengers that had only recently been included on the service.

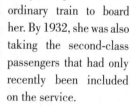

The SS *Canterbury* plied the English Channel for almost 35 years. Her final passenger sailing was on 27 September 1963, by which time British Railways were running the service. She had seen the high-life and exclusivity of the late 1920s and the hard times of the Depression and the Second World War. Having weathered many storms at sea and changes on land and finally, after having outlived the company that had commissioned her, the Southern Railway, by 15 years, she was sold and broken up in 1964.

Opposite top: A couple stroll along the deck of the Golden Arrow ferry, 1947
Opposite below: The night ferry train, 1930
Above: Passengers disembark a ferry from Dover to continue their journey to Paris, 1951

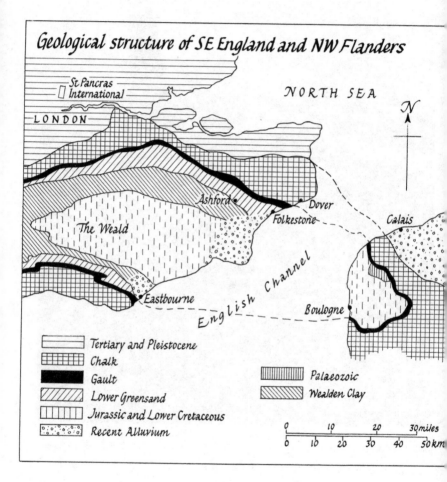

Geological structure of SE England and NW Flanders

St Pancras
International

LONDON

NORTH SEA

N

The Weald

Ashford

Dover

Folkestone

Calais

Eastbourne

English Channel

Boulogne

Tertiary and Pleistocene
Chalk
Gault
Lower Greensand
Jurassic and Lower Cretaceous
Recent Alluvium

Palaeozoic
Wealden Clay

0	10	20	30 miles
0	10	20	30	40	50 km

VIA THE CHANNEL TUNNEL

Entered half a mile after leaving Folkestone terminal the tunnel proceeds eastwards curving to the south-east as it descends below Shakespeare cliff turning a little more south-eastwards at mid-Channel, rising to enter France three miles inland beyond Sangatte, arriving at Calais-Frétun 166 km from London St Pancras.

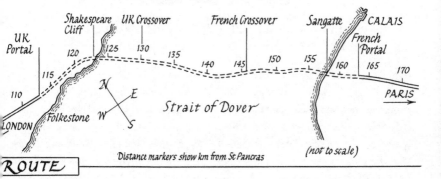

ROUTE — Distance markers show km from St Pancras

TWIN TUNNELS
(each single-tracked)

PRESSURE RELIEF DUCT

Service tunnel

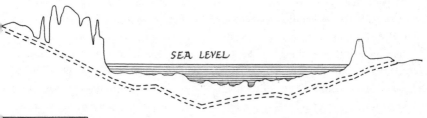

SEA LEVEL

PROFILE

(not to scale)

9a

The Channel Tunnel in History

On 1 December 1990, British and French flags were exchanged by workmen beneath the Channel as the Channel Tunnel breakthrough took place. Seventeen years later and Section 2 of HS1 was opened, allowing a train to make a single continuous journey from London to Paris. But the idea of a tunnel underneath the Channel was not a new one; for the best part of 200 years people had been planning, and even starting work on, tunnels that would connect Great Britain and France.

During the peace of Amiens in 1802–3, Napoleon Bonaparte expressed an interest in a French engineer's proposal to connect Britain and France via a tunnel. Informal discussions with a British diplomat took place but the scheme came to nothing as the two countries were quickly at war with each other again. Another French engineer suggested submerging a tube to the seabed in 1851 while, in 1855, the British engineer Wylson even put forward the idea of a floating tunnel anchored at each coast and supported with buoys along its length.

An Anglo-French consortium drew up serious plans for a tunnel in the 1860s that would have run from Dover to Sangatte, near Calais. They even got so far as to fund trial excavations but these do not appear to have progressed very far. By the 1870s the proposals began to be less speculative and far more grounded in exploiting the commercial advantages of a tunnel between the two countries. In 1872, Lord Grosvenor formed the Channel Tunnel Co. Ltd and began experimental borings but once more a lack of finance and support from existing railway companies such as the South Eastern and the London, Chatham and Dover meant that the plans never quite took off.

In the run-up to the First World War the idea of a Channel Tunnel was repeatedly raised in Great Britain, but the mood of the country, and in particular of government, was one of isolation and so no progress was made. While feelings towards such a project softened somewhat during the inter-war years, it was not until the 1950s, with the formation of the Channel Tunnel Study Group (CTSG), that things began to take off. In 1963, the government officially supported the idea of a Channel Tunnel for the first time although it was not until 1971 that British Rail set up a group to work on planning the project.

Margaret Thatcher and President François Mitterand signed the Treaty of Canterbury agreeing on a new tunnel proposal and in 1987, the Channel Tunnel Act was given Royal Assent.

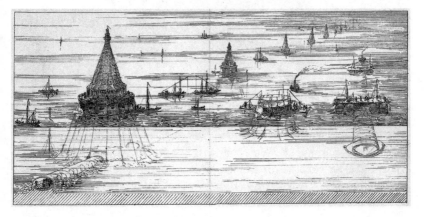

Despite such interest the project was abandoned in 1975, although an entrance to the first section had already been dug, as being too costly although within four years, further proposals for a tunnel were under consideration. It was in February 1984 that Prime Minister

Over 200 years of planning, proposals and setbacks had been overcome and, for the first time since the formation of the Channel over 200,000 years ago, Great Britain and France would be physically connected again.

Opposite: A French inventor proposed an amphibious train that would ride over the water, 1896
Above: An early depiction of a railway under the Channel Tunnel, 1851

Building the Channel Tunnel

As you travel beneath the English Channel on your way to Paris your thoughts might well turn to how exactly the tunnel was constructed. It is a singular feat of engineering that people had suggested and attempted for more than 100 years before it was finally achieved.

Work began in earnest in 1987 when vertical access shafts were constructed on both the French and English sides of the tunnel. The tunnels were dug using specially constructed Tunnel Boring Machines (TBMs) and 11 were needed to complete the project. Six of these worked from England and five from France. The TBMs were affectionately known as 'moles' and they consisted of a rotating cutting head at the front made up of hard disc cutters and a propulsion unit at the rear. The first of these machines cost £3.2 million to build in 1987 and had a diameter of 5.58 metres. It was capable of tunnelling at a rate of eight metres an hour. Three tunnels were dug, two wider

running tunnels and one narrower pilot, or service tunnel, and these required their own machines to excavate them.

The TBMs worked like a giant cheese grater as they moved through the chalk geology underneath the channel. They broke off the rock in manageable pieces, which were then collected immediately behind the cutter's head. This spoil was then moved out of the tunnel using huge Archimedes screws, conveyor belts and wagons. The machine was capable of moving itself along by using hydraulic gripper pads that pushed against the sides of the tunnel as it went.

Once the TBM had done its work, the tunnel then had to be lined with a strengthened concrete. The lining consisted of several segments that fitted together with a smaller 'key' piece to create a ring. On the English side the lining had eight segments, while on the French side it had five. The French side of the tunnel differed as it had to pass through more difficult geology and needed to be able to withstand greater pressures. These rings were moved into position along a specially constructed railway track and fitted using lifts and hoists. Once completed, the rings were pushed up against one another using massive hydraulic rams and the joints were then sealed.

The English and French tunnels united for the first time on 30 October 1990 and shortly afterwards the tunnels

were in the tunnel facing each other. Neither could reverse so the decision was taken to drive the slightly larger English TBM off to the side, creating a short side tunnel, into which the TBM was sealed forever in concrete.

There was a great deal of work still to be done on the tunnels before they could be open for traffic and it was not until 14 November 1994, four years after

were completed and the 50-km (31-mile) tunnel was open all the way through, from England to France. In total, 11 people died during the construction of the tunnel. Of course, when the tunnels met both the French and the English TBMs

the tunnels originally broke through, that the Channel Tunnel was opened for passenger services. It was estimated that over 170 million man-hours had gone into the construction of the tunnel.

Opposite top: An early indication of what the Channel Tunnel might look like, 1905
Opposite below: Work begins on the Channel Tunnel. It would take 170 million man-hours to complete
Above: Tunnellers celebrate following the breakthrough of the TBM onto the Eurotunnel UK terminal at Folkestone, 1990

Above: The SS *Canterbury* in the docks at Calais, 1929

Left: A couple have a drink at the famous bar on board the Golden Arrow, 1947

FLÈCHE D'OR

CALAIS MARITIME
103 miles from London

CALAIS

Gare Centrale

The Southern Railway put into commission six new cross-Channel steamers from 1923: *Dinard*, *St. Briac*, *Maid of Kent*, *Isle of Thanet*, *Worthing* and *Canterbury*. However, the SS *Canterbury*, built by William Denny Bros. of Dumbarton, was the only ship designed to be expressly for the use of the Golden Arrow service. The new service was inaugurated on 15 May 1929 and was a first-class service throughout. In 1929, the first-class single fare including all Pullman supplements on both sides of the Channel, was £5.

Strait of

Dover

Cross-Channel timetable – 1930

Leaves London Victoria............11.00 a.m.
Arrives Dover Marine Station......12.38 p.m.
Canterbury leaves Dover Marine....12.55 p.m.
Canterbury arrives Calais Maritime..2.10 p.m.
Flêche d'Or leaves Calais Maritime..2.25 p.m.
Arrives Paris Nord...............5.35 p.m.

(First-class single fare £5)

The SS *Canterbury* entered service in 1929 and a writer at the time commented that she was 'the last word in cross-Channel construction' and that 'no one is allowed to set foot upon her who has not a Golden Arrow ticket'. The Golden Arrow service that left Victoria at 11am would have been carrying fewer than 300 and the SS *Canterbury* accommodated such a small number with ease. She had a Garden Café in the stern and an oak-panelled smoking room, along with a Parisian-style restaurant where passengers could spend their time on board.

Dover Harbour

DOVER MARINE
77 miles from London

Dover Harbour Stn

(not to scale)

9

The Culture of Northern France

It is important to remember, while travelling through the countryside at over 180 mph, that the landscapes which pass by your window in a dizzying blur have a depth and character all of their own. Northern France is more than simply the sum of the battles that have been fought here over the years and it should not be seen simply as an unwelcome distance interposing itself between you and Paris.

There is a rich and colourful history to this region of France. It is called Picardy and the Eurostar travels through its beautiful capital Amiens. Aisne, Oise and Somme are the three 'Departments' that make up the region and the train passes through them all on its way to Paris. Much in the culture of Picardy has been influenced by its neighbour to the North, Belgium. In fact, while the language of Picard has not been officially recognised by the French government, over the border in Belgium it has. While there are similarities with French, Picard is distinctly different, having its own words and pronunciation and, while perhaps not spoken by everyone, it is still possible to hear Picard spoken in the countryside.

There is a rich tradition of folk songs in the language, which in the South of the region is also known as Chtimi. The region has a popular musical tradition which has helped to keep the language alive, and with it comes its own distinctive musical instrument: the pipasso. This is a small bagpipe similar to those traditionally played further west in Brittany.

There is also a bewildering array of alcoholic drinks for which the region is rightly famous and foremost among these is the local cider. It is lighter, not so strong as the traditional cider found in England and Wales, and has a much livelier sparkle. As in Kent, there are orchards, heavy with blossom or fruit depending on the season, punctuating the fields. Beekeeping has a long history in the region and the drink of hydromel, made from fermented honey, can be compared with the ancient beverage of mead. The Belgian influence is also in evidence, with a strong tradition of beer brewing.

Like all of France, the region has its

own speciality dishes and such a fertile area lends itself to high-quality meats and cheeses. The lamb from the salt marshes (the route of the Flèche d'Or passed through extensive salt marshes near the Bay of the Somme) is said to be particularly good, although perhaps the greatest culinary gift the region has bestowed upon the world is that of the sweet Chantilly cream.

Opposite: The cathedral in Amiens, first built in 1220
Above: The salt marshes at Picardy

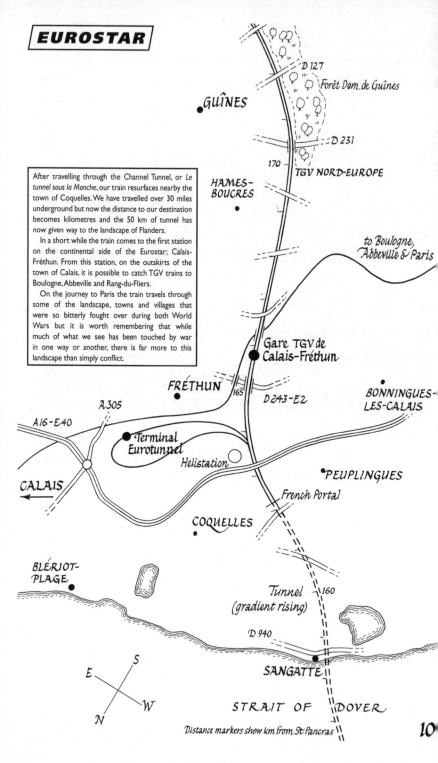

EUROSTAR

GUÎNES

D 127

Forêt Dom. de Guînes

D 231

170

TGV NORD-EUROPE

HAMES-BOUCRES

After travelling through the Channel Tunnel, or *Le tunnel sous la Manche*, our train resurfaces nearby the town of Coquelles. We have travelled over 30 miles underground but now the distance to our destination becomes kilometres and the 50 km of tunnel has now given way to the landscape of Flanders.

In a short while the train comes to the first station on the continental side of the Eurostar; Calais-Fréthun. From this station, on the outskirts of the town of Calais, it is possible to catch TGV trains to Boulogne, Abbeville and Rang-du-Fliers.

On the journey to Paris the train travels through some of the landscape, towns and villages that were so bitterly fought over during both World Wars but it is worth remembering that while much of what we see has been touched by war in one way or another, there is far more to this landscape than simply conflict.

to Boulogne, Abbeville & Paris

Gare TGV de
Calais-Fréthun

FRÉTHUN

165   D 243-E2

BONNINGUES-
LES-CALAIS

A 305

A 16 - E 40

Terminal
Eurotunnel

Helistation

PEUPLINGUES

CALAIS

French Portal

COQUELLES

BLÉRIOT-
PLAGE

Tunnel
(gradient rising)   160

D 940

S

E   SANGATTE

W

N

STRAIT OF   DOVER

Distance markers show km from St Pancras

10

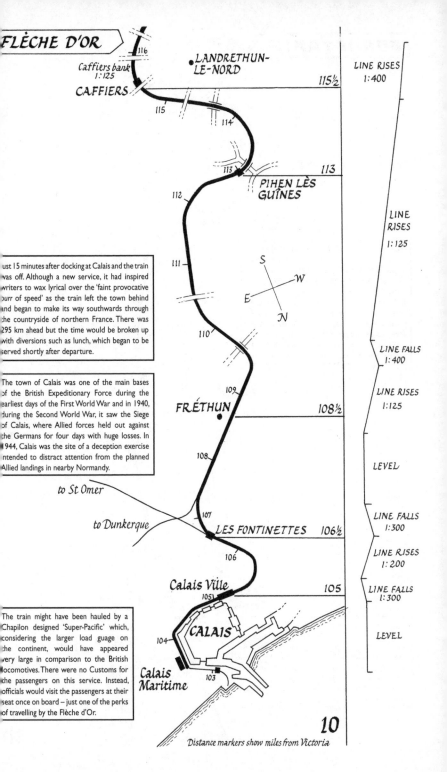

FLÈCHE D'OR

116

Caffiers bank
1:125

CAFFIERS

115

114

• LANDRETHUN-
LE-NORD

115½

113

113

PIHEN LÈS
GUÎNES

112

111

S

W

E

N

110

109

FRÉTHUN

108½

108

to St Omer

107

to Dunkerque

LES FONTINETTES   106½

106

Calais Ville

105

105

CALAIS

104

103

Calais
Maritime

LINE RISES
1:400

LINE
RISES
1:125

LINE FALLS
1:400

LINE RISES
1:125

LEVEL

LINE FALLS
1:300

LINE RISES
1:200

LINE FALLS
1:300

LEVEL

ust 15 minutes after docking at Calais and the train
was off. Although a new service, it had inspired
writers to wax lyrical over the 'faint provocative
purr of speed' as the train left the town behind
and began to make its way southwards through
the countryside of northern France. There was
295 km ahead but the time would be broken up
with diversions such as lunch, which began to be
served shortly after departure.

The town of Calais was one of the main bases
of the British Expeditionary Force during the
earliest days of the First World War and in 1940,
during the Second World War, it saw the Siege
of Calais, where Allied forces held out against
the Germans for four days with huge losses. In
1944, Calais was the site of a deception exercise
intended to distract attention from the planned
Allied landings in nearby Normandy.

The train might have been hauled by a
Chapilon designed 'Super-Pacific' which,
considering the larger load guage on
the continent, would have appeared
very large in comparison to the British
locomotives. There were no Customs for
the passengers on this service. Instead,
officials would visit the passengers at their
seat once on board – just one of the perks
of travelling by the Flèche d'Or.

10

Distance markers show miles from Victoria

EUROSTAR

D 218

D 217

A 26 - E 15

Autoroute
des Anglais

D 226

D 217

**TOURNEHEM-
SUR-LA-HEM**

D 943   185

**LA-GRANDE-
RUE**

D 225

E

N ✧ S

W

YEUSE

D 224   180

The train travels on at high speed through the
countryside. It passes first the Forest of Guînes
and then the woods by the small town of Licques
on the right-hand side before passing the small
town of Landrethun lès Ardres on the left.
About 7 km later, the Eurostar passes by
Tournehem-sur-la-Hem, a fortified town that is
built around the remains of a twelfth-century
château and also features the remains of
a fifteenth-century windmill.

The train passes under a series of roads before
making its way further eastwards towards Paris.

**LANDRETHUN-
LÈS-ARDRES**

**BOIS DE
LICQUES**

RODELINGHEM

D 215

**CAMPAGNE-
LÈS-GUÎNES**

175   **BOUQUEHAULT**

FORÊT DOM. DE GUÎNES

Around 6 km after leaving Calais-Fréthun, the train
passes by the town of Guînes to the East, on the
left-hand side. This town has a long history, being
occupied at least since Roman times. The town and the
surrounding countryside changed hands several times
during the medieval period. The English captured it in
the 1350s and held the town for 200 years until it was
recaptured by the French in the 1550s.

GUÎNES

11a

The Building of High Speed, Part Two

The building of the railway network that joined together the two countries was fraught with problems. In Britain, the new high-speed rail link (HS1) cut through some of the most beautiful landscape in the South of England. Meanwhile, in France, there were wider political and economic issues that had to be overcome.

Many of the tunnels along the route of High Speed 1 ensure that the Eurostar travels underneath such sensitive sites and causes as little damage as possible. The French railway network had already been extensively remodelled from the late 1960s. This meant that there was perhaps less strategic work to be done and, once opened in 1994, the Eurostar quickly took its place alongside the high-speed trains (TGV) that had been running in France for some years. But the history of the line is equally interesting and bound up with the politics of the 1970s and 80s.

The notion of a Europe-wide high-speed railway network came about at around the same time as Great Britain decided to join the European Economic Community in 1973. Several European countries, in particular West Germany, were interested in the economic possibilities that a Europe-wide high-speed rail network would open up. However, progress was slow and agreement between countries was difficult to reach. Margaret Thatcher and François Mitterand, the respective leaders of Great Britain and France, struggled through the early 1980s to reach an agreement about whether to use railways or a combination of road and rail. Finally they agreed and, in 1986, the project got underway in earnest.

In Britain there were often protests from groups of residents who did not want to see the line run through, and potentially destroy, landscapes they loved. There were many demonstrations and, because of this, a great deal of effort was taken to ensure that the impact of the line was minimised wherever possible. It is interesting to note that, in France, there were demonstrations because the line *did not* pass through a certain area. Residents of the city of Amiens were so incensed by the fact that the Eurostar would not pass through their city that they bought up land that was on the proposed route. They then resold it at rock-bottom prices to thousands of individual owners in an attempt to force the French government to reroute the line through their city.

The building of the railway and the tunnel on both sides of the Channel was complex and the financial arrangements between the companies involved were turbulent. However, the project was completed and the archaeological, environmental and, perhaps most importantly, political problems were eventually overcome.

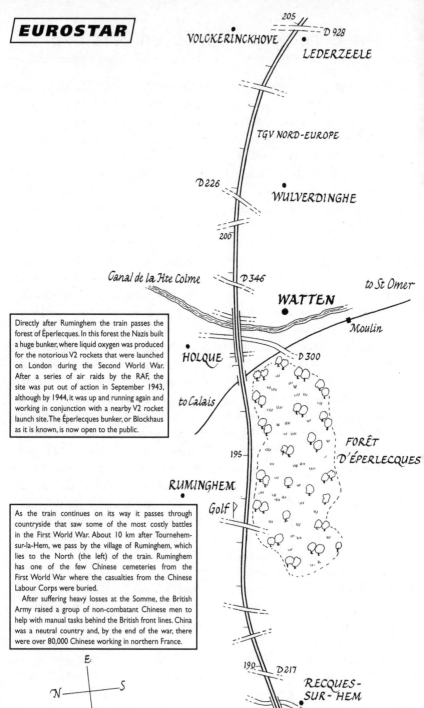

EUROSTAR

VOLCKERINCKHOVE

205 · D 928

LEDERZEELE

TGV NORD-EUROPE

D226

WULVERDINGHE

200

Canal de la Hte Colme · D346

WATTEN · to St Omer

Moulin

HOLQUE · D 300

to Calais

Directly after Ruminghem the train passes the forest of Éperlecques. In this forest the Nazis built a huge bunker, where liquid oxygen was produced for the notorious V2 rockets that were launched on London during the Second World War. After a series of air raids by the RAF, the site was put out of action in September 1943, although by 1944, it was up and running again and working in conjunction with a nearby V2 rocket launch site. The Éperlecques bunker, or Blockhaus as it is known, is now open to the public.

FORÊT D'ÉPERLECQUES

195

RUMINGHEM

Golf

As the train continues on its way it passes through countryside that saw some of the most costly battles in the First World War. About 10 km after Tournehem-sur-la-Hem, we pass by the village of Ruminghem, which lies to the North (the left) of the train. Ruminghem has one of the few Chinese cemeteries from the First World War where the casualties from the Chinese Labour Corps were buried.

After suffering heavy losses at the Somme, the British Army raised a group of non-combatant Chinese men to help with manual tasks behind the British front lines. China was a neutral country and, by the end of the war, there were over 80,000 Chinese working in northern France.

E

N — S

W

190 · D217

RECQUES-SUR-HEM

12a

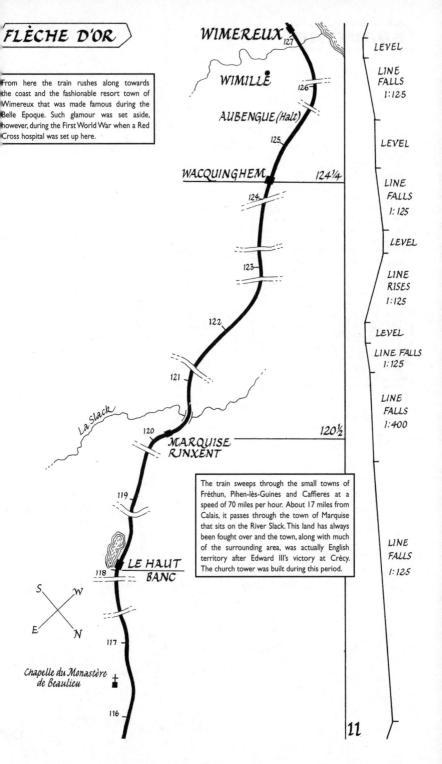

FLÈCHE D'OR

From here the train rushes along towards the coast and the fashionable resort town of Wimereux that was made famous during the Belle Epoque. Such glamour was set aside, however, during the First World War when a Red Cross hospital was set up here.

WIMEREUX 127

WIMILLE 126

AUBENGUE (Halt) 125

WACQUINGHEM 124¼

124

123

122

121

La Slack 120

MARQUISE RINXENT 120½

119

LE HAUT BANC 118

117

Chapelle du Monastère de Beaulieu

116

The train sweeps through the small towns of Fréthun, Pihen-lès-Guines and Caffieres at a speed of 70 miles per hour. About 17 miles from Calais, it passes through the town of Marquise that sits on the River Slack. This land has always been fought over and the town, along with much of the surrounding area, was actually English territory after Edward III's victory at Crécy. The church tower was built during this period.

LEVEL

LINE FALLS 1:125

LEVEL

LINE FALLS 1:125

LEVEL

LINE RISES 1:125

LEVEL

LINE FALLS 1:125

LINE FALLS 1:400

LINE FALLS 1:125

11

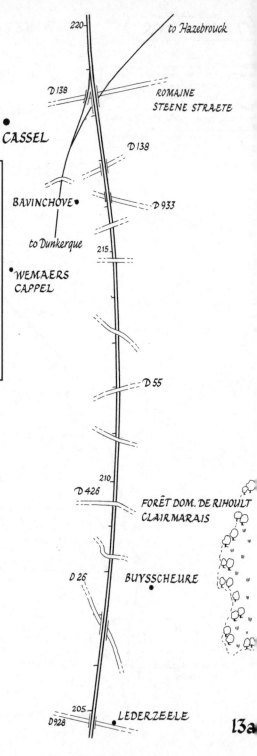

220

to Hazebrouck

D 138

ROMAINE
STEENE STRAETE

CASSEL

D 138

The train passes by the towns of Watten and Lederzeele before entering a long straight stretch of track that runs for 15 km towards the town of Cassel. Cassel is a distinctive town, especially amid the flat landscape of Flanders, in that it is built on the top of a hill that is over 170 metres above sea level. It is thought that this is the hill in the nursery rhyme 'The Grand Old Duke of York' and refers to Frederick, the Duke of York, second son of George III, who failed to take the town in the Flanders Campaign of 1793–94, although there is no direct proof of this.

The town's location, on such a prominent hill, means that it was settled from the Roman period. Well before the Flanders Campaign it was the site of violent battles from the ninth century right up to the Second World War, when much of it was destroyed. Cassel has now been extensively rebuilt and boasts many hotels, cafes and restaurants.

BAVINCHOVE•

D 933

to Dunkerque

215

•WEMAERS
CAPPEL

D 55

210

D 426

FORÊT DOM. DE RIHOULT
CLAIRMARAIS

D 26

BUYSSCHEURE

E

S

N

W

205

LEDERZEELE

D 928

13a

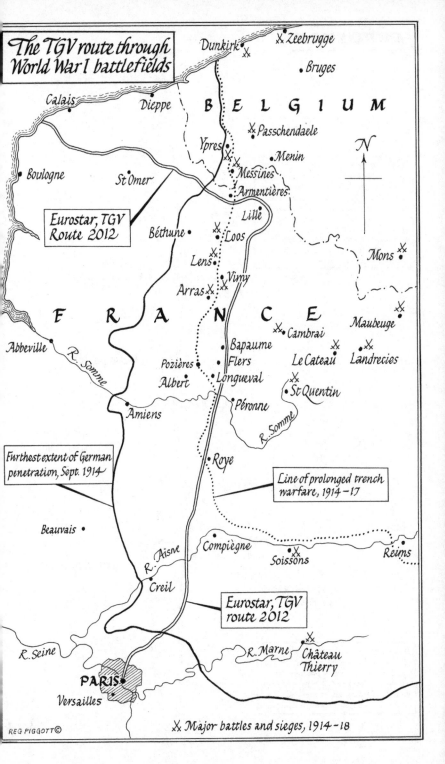

The TGV route through World War I battlefields

Dunkirk
Zeebrugge
Bruges

B E L G I U M

Calais
Dieppe

Passchendaele

Ypres
Menin

Boulogne
St Omer
Messines
Armentières

N

Eurostar, TGV Route 2012

Lille

Béthune
Loos

F R A N C E

Lens

Arras
Vimy

Mons

Maubeuge

Abbeville
R. Somme

Bapaume
Cambrai

Le Cateau
Landrecies

Pozières
Flers

Albert
Longueval

St Quentin

Péronne

R. Somme

Amiens

Furthest extent of German penetration, Sept. 1914

Roye

Line of prolonged trench warfare, 1914–17

Beauvais

Compiègne

Reims

R. Aisne
Soissons

Creil

Eurostar, TGV route 2012

R. Marne
Château Thierry

R. Seine

PARIS

Versailles

REG PIGGOTT©

✗✗ Major battles and sieges, 1914–18

EUROSTAR

to Lille

235
D 23

OUTTERSTEENE

MÉTEREN

MERRIS

The train continues on its way Southeast through the countryside past the town of Strazeele on the right-hand side, which is known for its equestrian activity, and on towards Méteren. The town of Méteren has a First World War cemetery that contains the graves of troops from both sides of the conflict. Bodies of soldiers from Great Britain, Canada, Australia, New Zealand and India are all buried here, along with many French casualties.

Monts de Flandre

D 642

TGV NORD-EUROPE

D 947

230
FLÊTRE

STRAZEELE

D 642

D 947

PRADELLES

CAESTRE 227

FORÊT ET
DOM. DE NIEPPE

225
D 161

D 916

HAZEBROUCK

ST-SYLVESTRE-
CAPPEL

HONDEGHEM

The landscape of Flanders is filled with stories of wars and fighting. To the right, the train passes by the small town of Hondeghem, which was the scene of particularly heavy fighting as a Royal Horse Artillery battery attempted to fight off an attack by the German Army in May 1940.

D 53

E

N — S

W

14a

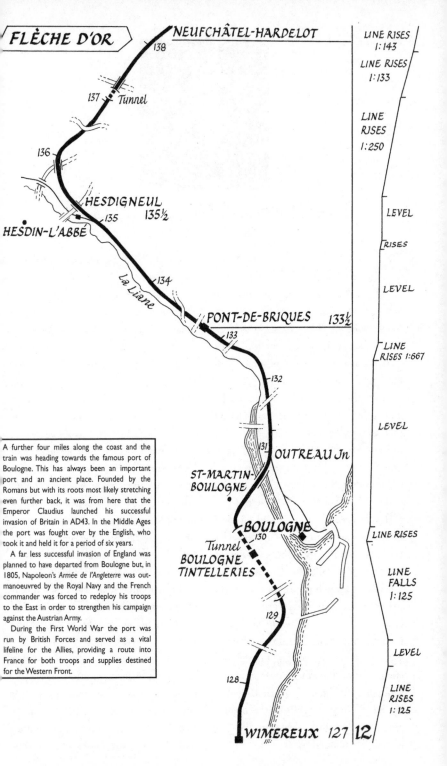

FLÈCHE D'OR

NEUFCHÂTEL-HARDELOT
138

LINE RISES 1:143

LINE RISES 1:133

137 Tunnel

LINE RISES 1:250

136

HESDIGNEUL 135½
135

HESDIN-L'ABBÉ

LEVEL

RISES

La Liane
134

LEVEL

PONT-DE-BRIQUES 133½
133

LINE RISES 1:667

132

131 OUTREAU Jn

LEVEL

ST-MARTIN-BOULOGNE

BOULOGNE
130

LINE RISES

Tunnel
BOULOGNE TINTELLERIES

LINE FALLS 1:125

129

LEVEL

128

LINE RISES 1:125

WIMEREUX 127 | 12

A further four miles along the coast and the train was heading towards the famous port of Boulogne. This has always been an important port and an ancient place. Founded by the Romans but with its roots most likely stretching even further back, it was from here that the Emperor Claudius launched his successful invasion of Britain in AD43. In the Middle Ages the port was fought over by the English, who took it and held it for a period of six years.

A far less successful invasion of England was planned to have departed from Boulogne but, in 1805, Napoleon's *Armée de l'Angleterre* was out-manoeuvred by the Royal Navy and the French commander was forced to redeploy his troops to the East in order to strengthen his campaign against the Austrian Army.

During the First World War the port was run by British Forces and served as a vital lifeline for the Allies, providing a route into France for both troops and supplies destined for the Western Front.

Literature and Northern France

There is a rich culture in Northern France with its own identity and traditions. It has also inspired many novelists over the years and there are strong links between the region and some of the country's most famous writers. Reading while on a train has been a favourite pastime since the middle of the nineteenth century. W.H. Smith began life selling books and periodicals to passengers on station platforms in the nineteenth century. But the choice of book is important and, armed with a little knowledge about the literature that relates to the region, making this choice can be easier.

Émile Zola always insisted on field research when writing his novels. His book *Germinal*, from 1885, is set at the time of a strike by coal miners in a northern French town. For this work, part of a much larger series of novels called *Les Rougon-Macquart*, he visited the town of Anzin. The Eurostar spends much of its journey moving through the coalfields of Picardy and this novel, while uncompromising in its portrayal of the harsh realities of life in the region, might be the ideal companion for the historically minded reader.

Another writer who captured northern France in his work was Marcel Proust. While he was born in Paris, the opening sequences of the first volume of his famous series of novels *À La Recherche Du Temps Perdu* (or *In Search of Lost Time*) from 1913 was set in the northern town of Combray, just to the Southwest of Paris. He actually based the place in the novel on the small town of Illiers and it is here that he describes the famous memories of the Madeleines, or sweet cakes, made by his aunt that he remembered from his youth. In honour of the novelist, and his influence, the town changed its name to that of Illiers-Combray. While not on the route of the Eurostar, the scenes of rural town life that Proust describes have a resonance throughout the region.

Proust published the first volume of the series in the year before the outbreak of the First World War. While naturally bloody and destructive, a generation of writers and poets found the war a grim inspiration and wrote some of the most moving novels and verse in the English language. The War Poets, as they are known, included Rupert Brooke, who died in 1915, Edward Thomas, who wrote the famous railway poem, *Adlestrop*, and was killed in 1917, and Wilfred Owen. Owen is possibly the most famous of the War Poets and his work is still widely read today. One of the most powerful of his works is *Dulce Et Decorum Est*, an attack on those who thought war a noble enterprise. He was killed in 1918 in the woods of Compiègne, just seven days before the signing of the Armistice, which ended the war.

Other writers survived the war and went on to produce books that are today considered to be masterpieces. Robert Graves' autobiographical account of the war, *Goodbye to All That* from 1926, is just one example, while Siegfried Sassoon's First World War trilogy, including *Memoirs of a Fox-Hunting Man* from 1928, is another.

More recently, Pat Barker's *Regeneration* trilogy (1991–95) has continued the literary associations with the First World War and northern France; in it, Siegfried Sassoon appears as a character. Sebastian Faulks' *Birdsong* from 1993, which deals with the war in great detail, is set in part in the city of Amiens (on the route of the Flèche d'Or). *Birdsong* was made into a BBC TV drama in 2012.

There is a great deal of choice for the railway traveller who, relaxing in their seat, wants to while away an hour with a good book. As the countryside flashes by, what this landscape has inspired in the way of literature might seem surprising.

Opposite: Marcel Proust, 1871–1922
Above: Honoré de Balzac, 1799–1850

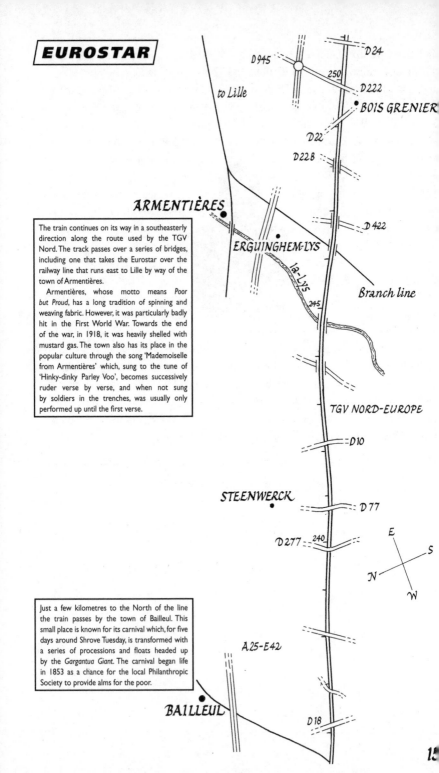

EUROSTAR

to Lille

D 945

250

D 24

D 222

● BOIS GRENIER

D 22

D 22B

ARMENTIÈRES ●

D 422

The train continues on its way in a southeasterly direction along the route used by the TGV Nord. The track passes over a series of bridges, including one that takes the Eurostar over the railway line that runs east to Lille by way of the town of Armentières.

Armentières, whose motto means *Poor but Proud*, has a long tradition of spinning and weaving fabric. However, it was particularly badly hit in the First World War. Towards the end of the war, in 1918, it was heavily shelled with mustard gas. The town also has its place in the popular culture through the song 'Mademoiselle from Armentières' which, sung to the tune of 'Hinky-dinky Parley Voo', becomes successively ruder verse by verse, and when not sung by soldiers in the trenches, was usually only performed up until the first verse.

ERGUINGHEM-LYS ●

la Lys

245

Branch line

TGV NORD-EUROPE

D 10

STEENWERCK ●

D 77

D 277 240

E

S

N

W

Just a few kilometres to the North of the line the train passes by the town of Bailleul. This small place is known for its carnival which, for five days around Shrove Tuesday, is transformed with a series of processions and floats headed up by the *Gargantua Giant*. The carnival began life in 1853 as a chance for the local Philanthropic Society to provide alms for the poor.

A 25-E42

BAILLEUL ●

D 18

1

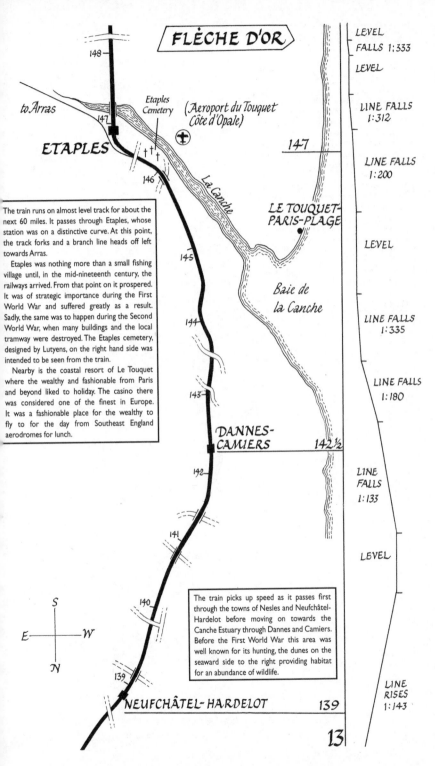

FLÈCHE D'OR

148

to Arras

147

ETAPLES

146

Etaples
Cemetery

(Aeroport du Touquet
Côte d'Opale)

☩

† † †

La Canche

147

LEVEL
FALLS 1:333

LEVEL

LINE FALLS
1:312

LINE FALLS
1:200

LE TOUQUET-
PARIS-PLAGE

145

LEVEL

144

Baie de
la Canche

143

DANNES-
CAMIERS

142½

LINE FALLS
1:335

LINE FALLS
1:180

142

LINE
FALLS
1:133

141

LEVEL

140

S

E ——— W

N

139

LINE
RISES
1:143

NEUFCHÂTEL-HARDELOT   139

13

The train runs on almost level track for about the next 60 miles. It passes through Etaples, whose station was on a distinctive curve. At this point, the track forks and a branch line heads off left towards Arras.

Etaples was nothing more than a small fishing village until, in the mid-nineteenth century, the railways arrived. From that point on it prospered. It was of strategic importance during the First World War and suffered greatly as a result. Sadly, the same was to happen during the Second World War, when many buildings and the local tramway were destroyed. The Etaples cemetery, designed by Lutyens, on the right hand side was intended to be seen from the train.

Nearby is the coastal resort of Le Touquet where the wealthy and fashionable from Paris and beyond liked to holiday. The casino there was considered one of the finest in Europe. It was a fashionable place for the wealthy to fly to for the day from Southeast England aerodromes for lunch.

The train picks up speed as it passes first through the towns of Nesles and Neufchâtel-Hardelot before moving on towards the Canche Estuary through Dannes and Camiers. Before the First World War this area was well known for its hunting, the dunes on the seaward side to the right providing habitat for an abundance of wildlife.

About 20 km on from Armentières the train arrives at Lille, the first station stop and large city since Calais. Lille was, like so many towns and cities in northern France, extensively rebuilt after the two World Wars and is now very proud of its restored Old Quarter.

The town has a history that goes back over 1,000 years and archaeological excavations have suggested that there may have been settlement here in prehistoric times. These days the city has a reputation for being something of a cultural centre and there are many museums and galleries in the city centre. Charles de Gaulle was born in Lille in 1890 and his birthplace is now a museum dedicated to his life. While many have judged the architecture of the city to be typical of the area, the façade of the Cathedral – built in 1999 – is striking in its modernism.

There are many cafes, bars and restaurants in Lille and the city's proximity to the border means that much of the food is heavily influenced by Dutch traditions.

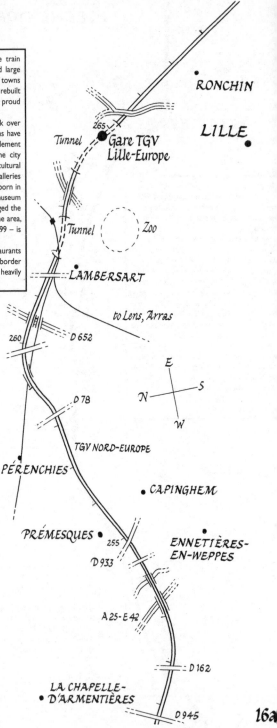

16a

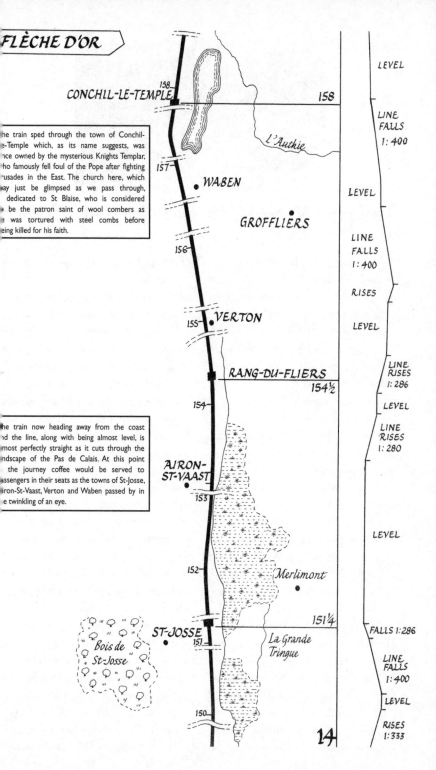

FLÈCHE D'OR

CONCHIL-LE-TEMPLE

158

158

157

L'Authie

WABEN

GROFFLIERS

156

VERTON

155

RANG-DU-FLIERS

154½

154

AIRON-ST-VAAST

153

152

Merlimont

151¼

ST-JOSSE

Bois de
St-Josse

151

La Grande
Tringue

150

The train sped through the town of Conchil-le-Temple which, as its name suggests, was once owned by the mysterious Knights Templar, who famously fell foul of the Pope after fighting Crusades in the East. The church here, which may just be glimpsed as we pass through, dedicated to St Blaise, who is considered to be the patron saint of wool combers as he was tortured with steel combs before being killed for his faith.

The train now heading away from the coast and the line, along with being almost level, is almost perfectly straight as it cuts through the landscape of the Pas de Calais. At this point the journey coffee would be served to passengers in their seats as the towns of St-Josse, Airon-St-Vaast, Verton and Waben passed by in the twinkling of an eye.

LEVEL

LINE
FALLS
1:400

LEVEL

LINE
FALLS
1:400

RISES

LEVEL

LINE
RISES
1:286

LEVEL

LINE
RISES
1:280

LEVEL

LEVEL

FALLS 1:286

LINE
FALLS
1:400

LEVEL

RISES
1:333

14

The First World War and Northern France

As we travel through northern France on the Eurostar it is easy to forget about the conflicts that have been played out in this otherwise quiet and essentially rural landscape. Famous battles such as Agincourt and Crécy were fought here many centuries ago; these were followed by more bloodshed in the form of the French Revolution and the Franco-Prussian War, but it was not until 1914 that modern warfare was unleashed on this otherwise unassuming region.

The outbreak of the First World War saw German forces quickly engaged in a 'Race to the Sea', which saw them occupy huge swathes of France in an attempt to get to the Atlantic coast. While the war began as a mobile affair, it quickly developed into a static conflict, with troops on both sides dug into heavily fortified trench systems. There were many reasons for this but, in the main, the technology of warfare had developed so much since the late nineteenth century that the tactics of pitched battles and the movement of large numbers of troops became virtually impossible. The development of the machine gun and the widespread use of barbed wire meant that the tactics employed by generals at the time were outdated and ineffective.

For the next three years the fighting was fierce, with neither side able to strike a decisive blow. It was not until 1917 that the tide would eventually turn against Germany. The naval blockade of Germany and her territories by the British Navy was beginning to have a serious impact on its ability to produce arms and armour for the war effort and food shortages were becoming increasingly serious. Germany's answer was to increase the submarine attacks on civilian and military shipping, which, in turn, brought the United States into the war. Although Germany had signed a peace treaty with Russia, which released troops to fight on the Western Front, the combination of a lack of resources along with the influx of American troops and materiel was to prove decisive. Despite the initial success of the German Spring Offensive of 1918, the Allied forces began to gain the upper hand and, on 11 November 1918, the Armistice was signed in a railway carriage in the forest of Compiègne only miles from the route of the Flèche d'Or.

Throughout much of the First World War, northern France was on the frontline. Our route takes us past some of the landscapes whose names have become synonymous with that conflict. The Somme stands out as the battle in which the British Army suffered its greatest-ever losses in a single day: 57,000 men were casualties and of these, well over 19,000 died. All of this took place on the first day of the Battle of the Somme, which began at 7.30am on 1 July 1916.

But this was only the first day of a battle that would last until 14 November 1916 and would see only meagre gains for the Allied forces. The landscape through which the Eurostar travels today was transformed into a wilderness of shattered trees and shell holes by the artillery on both sides. When the Flèche d'Or passed through France in the early 1930s the countryside and villages would still have been scarred by the fierce fighting; now those scars have healed. But even today, beneath the surface of these quiet fields, farmers still turn up hundreds of unexploded shells when they plough – a reminder of the lives lost and changed forever by the Great War.

Opposite: Horses pull ammunition through the mud to the forward guns at the Battle of the Somme, 1916
Above: An armoured train mounted with 190 calibre cannons, 1918

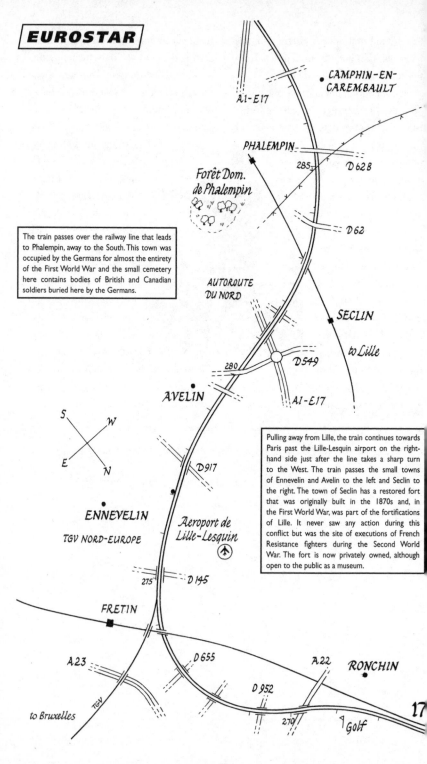

EUROSTAR

CAMPHIN-EN-CAREMBAULT

A1-E17

PHALEMPIN

285

D 62 B

Forêt Dom. de Phalempin

D 62

The train passes over the railway line that leads to Phalempin, away to the South. This town was occupied by the Germans for almost the entirety of the First World War and the small cemetery here contains bodies of British and Canadian soldiers buried here by the Germans.

AUTOROUTE DU NORD

SECLIN

to Lille

280

D549

AVELIN

A1-E17

S   W

E   N

D917

ENNEVELIN

TGV NORD-EUROPE

Aeroport de Lille-Lesquin

Pulling away from Lille, the train continues towards Paris past the Lille-Lesquin airport on the right-hand side just after the line takes a sharp turn to the West. The train passes the small towns of Ennevelin and Avelin to the left and Seclin to the right. The town of Seclin has a restored fort that was originally built in the 1870s and, in the First World War, was part of the fortifications of Lille. It never saw any action during this conflict but was the site of executions of French Resistance fighters during the Second World War. The fort is now privately owned, although open to the public as a museum.

275   D 145

FRETIN

A 23

D 655

A 22

RONCHIN

D 952

to Bruxelles

TGV

270

Golf

17

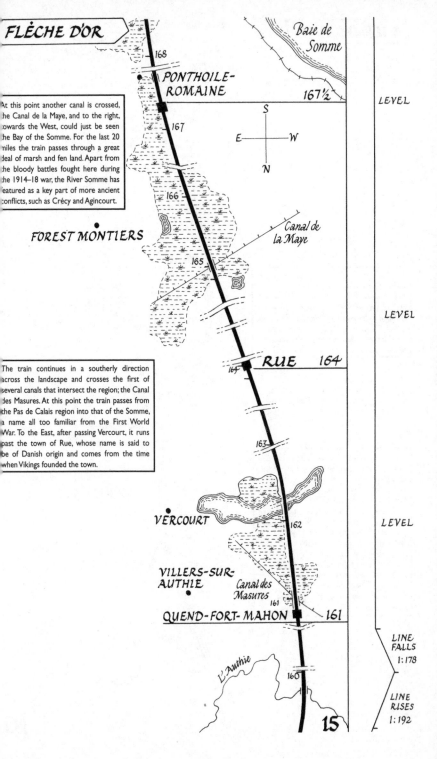

FLÈCHE D'OR

At this point another canal is crossed, the Canal de la Maye, and to the right, towards the West, could just be seen the Bay of the Somme. For the last 20 miles the train passes through a great deal of marsh and fen land. Apart from the bloody battles fought here during the 1914–18 war, the River Somme has featured as a key part of more ancient conflicts, such as Crécy and Agincourt.

The train continues in a southerly direction across the landscape and crosses the first of several canals that intersect the region; the Canal des Masures. At this point the train passes from the Pas de Calais region into that of the Somme, a name all too familiar from the First World War. To the East, after passing Vercourt, it runs past the town of Rue, whose name is said to be of Danish origin and comes from the time when Vikings founded the town.

Baie de Somme

168

PONTHOILE-ROMAINE

167½

LEVEL

167

166

FOREST MONTIERS

S

E — W

N

Canal de la Maye

165

164   RUE   164

LEVEL

163

162

VERCOURT

LEVEL

VILLERS-SUR-AUTHIE

Canal des Masures

161

QUEND-FORT-MAHON   161

L'Authie

160

15

LINE FALLS 1:178

LINE RISES 1:192

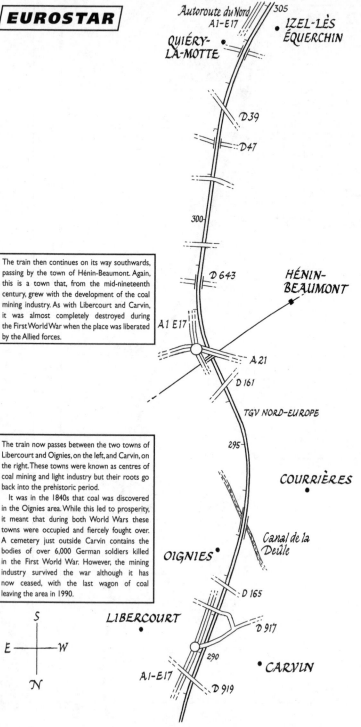

Autoroute du Nord
A1–E17
305
IZEL-LÈS ÉQUERCHIN

QUIÉRY-LA-MOTTE

D39

D47

300

D643

HÉNIN-BEAUMONT

A1 E17

A21

D161

TGV NORD–EUROPE

295

COURRIÈRES

Canal de la Deûle

OIGNIES

D165

LIBERCOURT

D917

S

E — W

N

A1–E17

290

D919

CARVIN

The train then continues on its way southwards, passing by the town of Hénin-Beaumont. Again, this is a town that, from the mid-nineteenth century, grew with the development of the coal mining industry. As with Libercourt and Carvin, it was almost completely destroyed during the First World War when the place was liberated by the Allied forces.

The train now passes between the two towns of Libercourt and Oignies, on the left, and Carvin, on the right. These towns were known as centres of coal mining and light industry but their roots go back into the prehistoric period.

It was in the 1840s that coal was discovered in the Oignies area. While this led to prosperity, it meant that during both World Wars these towns were occupied and fiercely fought over. A cemetery just outside Carvin contains the bodies of over 6,000 German soldiers killed in the First World War. However, the mining industry survived the war although it has now ceased, with the last wagon of coal leaving the area in 1990.

18a

FLÈCHE D'OR

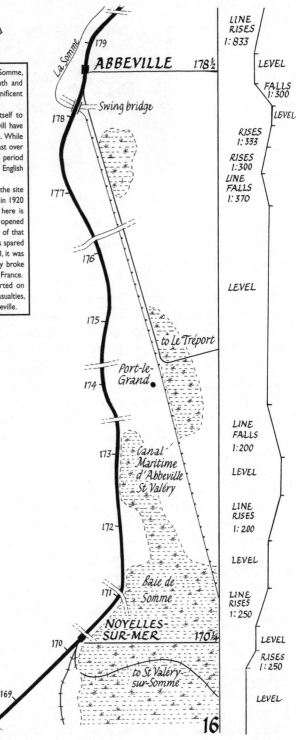

As the train skirts around the Bay of the Somme, the line takes a sharp turn to the South and heads along the track towards the magnificent town of Ábbeville at over 70 mph.

Ábbeville has much to recommend itself to the traveller but on this occasion, we will have to satisfy ourselves with but a glimpse. While this town has its roots far back in the past over 2,000 years ago, it was in the medieval period that it flourished, passing from French to English and then, finally, into Burgundian hands.

In the First World War the town was the site of a military hospital. Indeed, it was only in 1920 that the hospital closed. The cemetery here is one of the earliest from the war, having opened in 1914. It is a reminder of the horrors of that war but, a small mercy this, the town was spared serious bomb damage. However, in 1940, it was the point from which the German Army broke through French lines during the Battle of France.

The Battle of the Somme, which started on 1st July 1916, resulting in nearly 60,000 casualties, took place just over 20 miles East of Abbeville.

La Somme

179

ABBEVILLE   178½

Swing bridge

178

177

176

175

to Le Tréport

Port-le-Grand

174

173

Canal Maritime d'Abbeville St Valéry

172

Baie de Somme

171

NOYELLES-SUR-MER   170¼

170

to St Valéry-sur-Somme

169

16

LINE RISES 1:833

LEVEL

FALLS 1:300

LEVEL

RISES 1:333

RISES 1:300

LINE FALLS 1:370

LEVEL

LINE FALLS 1:200

LEVEL

LINE RISES 1:200

LEVEL

LINE RISES 1:250

LEVEL

RISES 1:250

LEVEL

The Railways of France

The French railway network is now considered to be among the most sophisticated in Europe. The TGV, or Train à Grande Vitesse, and the Eurostar certainly mean that France arguably has more than its fair share of high-speed, and similarly high-status, services. But this was not always the case; the French railway system was slow to develop and never grew at the rate that was seen in other countries such as Great Britain.

While engineers such as Marc Seguin were working on locomotive designs in the 1820s, the first railway in France opened in 1832, only seven years after the Stockton and Darlington Railway in the North of England. But after this, rather than the great explosion in railway building experienced in Great Britain, otherwise known as the 'railway mania', things moved rather more slowly in France. The upheaval of the Napoleonic Wars had left the country in a disorganised state and there was more required in the way of rebuilding rather than building new, and potentially risky, railways. France, with its large waterways, had always relied heavily on canals to transport

goods around the country. As such, the railways were considered to have been a serious threat to the already significant investment that many had made into the canal system.

Coupled with this was the fact that France was not so quick to industrialise as countries such as Great Britain. In the North of England private investors, who had already made large sums in industry, were happy to put up the necessary money to finance the railways. The predominantly rural nature of much of France meant that there simply were not as many willing to speculate such sums of money and those who were, were mainly based in Paris.

By the middle of the nineteenth century, government backing and financial support meant that there were a handful of large companies who operated the railway network. But government influence and the Paris-based nature of the investors meant that the network was largely made up of unconnected lines that radiated from the capital. This was to prove a serious problem in the Franco-Prussian War of the early

1870s as it was very difficult for the French forces to be moved around the country efficiently.

However, from these complicated beginnings the railway system grew until, by 1914, there was well over 35,000 miles of track. This dense railway network was vital during the First World War and both sides made extensive use of it. Huge sections of track were destroyed and many hundreds of miles

1938 with the creation of the Société Nationale des Chemins de fer Français (SNCF) and following further upheaval during the Second World War, which saw the railways in France used to transport many thousands to concentration camps, SNCF set about creating both an effective and sustainable railway network for the country.

These days, SNCF is seen as something of a market leader in the

of temporary track laid down by troops to allow for the movement of men and ammunition. Following the Armistice, the French railway network began to benefit from the reparations with Germany in the form of motive power and rolling stock, but despite this, the railways did not thrive. They were nationalised in

railway world and it has employees and consultants operating across the globe to provide advice and expertise to the railway builders of other nations. This is all a long way from France's uncertain first foray into the world of railways, 180 years ago.

Opposite: Even for the most well-off travellers comfort was not always a guarantee
Above: Passengers waiting to board the train in Paris, 1922

The train now passes under the railway line that runs southwest to the town of Arras. Arras has a long history and flourished in the medieval period. It is, however, for the battles that took place here during the First World War that the town has become most famous.

In May 1917 a combined force of British, New Zealand and Canadian troops attacked the German line. Although advances were made, once the battle was over the stalemate that characterised much of the trench warfare of the period continued for some time. The tactics used by the Allies included tunnelling and the experimental use of different types of artillery fire, such as the creeping barrage.

About 14 km after Hénin-Beaumont the train passes by the town of Gavrelle on the right-hand side to the Northwest. Gavrelle lies only a short distance from the town of Arras and was itself the scene of heavy fighting in the First World War. After several attempts by other regiments, the Royal Marines – who suffered their highest casualties of the war – captured the town and its windmill in 1917. Four Victoria Crosses were awarded to the regiment as a result of this action.

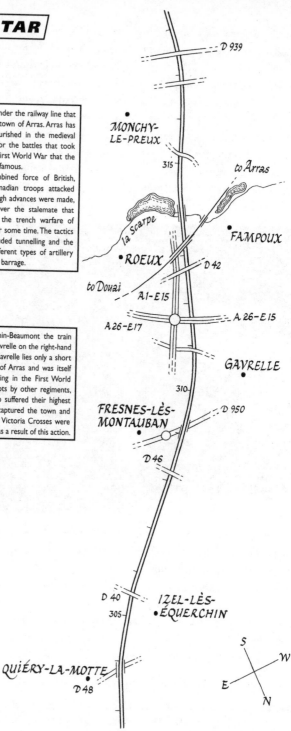

19a

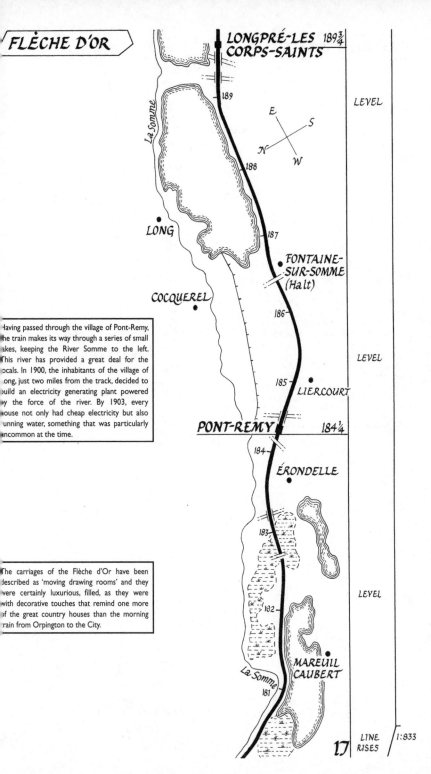

FLÈCHE D'OR

LONGPRÉ-LES 189¾
CORPS-SAINTS

189

LEVEL

188

LONG

187

FONTAINE-
SUR-SOMME
(Halt)

COCQUEREL

186

LEVEL

185

LIERCOURT

PONT-REMY 184¼

184

ÉRONDELLE

183

182

LEVEL

MAREUIL
CAUBERT

181

Having passed through the village of Pont-Remy, the train makes its way through a series of small lakes, keeping the River Somme to the left. This river has provided a great deal for the locals. In 1900, the inhabitants of the village of Long, just two miles from the track, decided to build an electricity generating plant powered by the force of the river. By 1903, every house not only had cheap electricity but also running water, something that was particularly uncommon at the time.

The carriages of the Flèche d'Or have been described as 'moving drawing rooms' and they were certainly luxurious, filled, as they were with decorative touches that remind one more of the great country houses than the morning train from Orpington to the City.

17 LINE 1:833
RISES

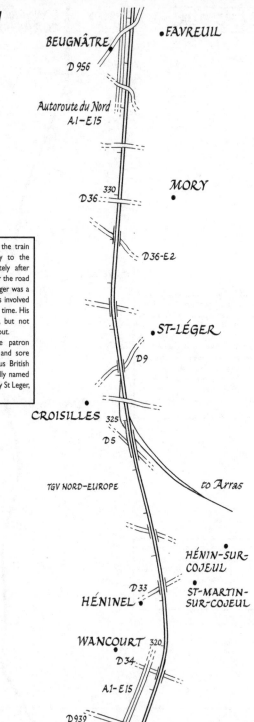

About 10 km further along the line the train passes another spur that runs away to the North-west towards Arras. Immediately after this the track runs across a bridge over the road to the small town of St-Léger. Saint Léger was a local Bishop who, in the late 660s, was involved in the political power struggles of the time. His adversaries eventually murdered him, but not before he had his eyes and tongue cut out.

Unsurprisingly, Saint Léger is the patron saint of protection against blindness and sore eyes, as well as of millers. The famous British horse race of the same name is actually named after its founder, Major General Anthony St Leger, and not for the saint.

20a

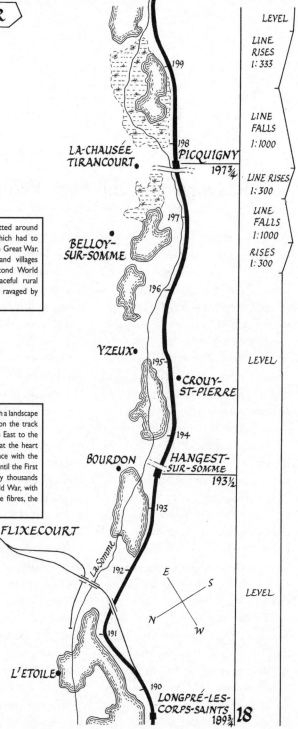

There are many small villages dotted around this landscape, the majority of which had to rebuilt almost entirely after the Great War. Similarly, many of these towns and villages were badly damaged in the Second World War. What appears to be a peaceful rural landscape has, in fact, been twice ravaged by war in the last century.

The train continues southeast through a landscape dotted with lakes and fens. Very soon the track splits and a branch heads off to the East to the town of Flixecourt. Flixecourt was at the heart of the Industrial Revolution in France with the development of the jute trade and until the First World War, had factories staffed by thousands of workers. After the Second World War, with the introduction of more man-made fibres, the industry began to rapidly decline.

LEVEL

LINE RISES 1:333

LINE FALLS 1:1000

LA-CHAUSÉE TIRANCOURT   PICQUIGNY
199
198
197¾
LINE RISES 1:300

LINE FALLS 1:1000

BELLOY-SUR-SOMME
197

196
RISES 1:300

YZEUX
195
LEVEL

CROUY-ST-PIERRE

194

BOURDON   HANGEST-SUR-SOMME
193½

193

FLIXECOURT

La Somme

192
E
S
N
W
LEVEL

191

L'ETOILE

190
LONGPRÉ-LES-CORPS-SAINTS
189¾   **18**

Railways and the First World War

While travelling through this part of France it is impossible not to be aware of the impact of the two world wars. A traveller on the Eurostar is literally surrounded by the legacy of those conflicts, whether or not they are aware of it. Similarly, a traveller on the Flèche d'Or during the inter-war period, although travelling along a different route, would have been just as immersed in the remains of the First World War but in this case the evidence would have been all around as the landscape bore the scars of the fighting for many years after the Armistice.

It is important not to overlook the role that railways played in the fighting on the Western Front between 1914 and 1918. The railways had become increasingly important in modern warfare from their first use in the Crimean War in the mid-1850s to the decisive role they played in the Franco-Prussian War of the early 1870s. But, in the First World War, they were essential in allowing troops and materiel to be moved around quickly and in bulk. Commentators at the time described the opening months of the war in 1914

as 'war by timetable', such was the part played by the railways.

The landscape of the war in northern France was mainly flat and low-lying, meaning that railways were ideally suited to the movement of troops and materiel. Therefore, railways were used on both sides. In 1915, the British Army formed the Railway Operating Department (ROD) as part of the Royal Engineers and hired locomotives from the Belgian Government to operate on the continent. The ROD eventually ended up with large numbers of locomotives requisitioned from railway companies in Britain and photographs of the period show familiar engines in very unfamiliar surroundings.

The ROD were involved with relaying tracks that had been destroyed by bombing and operating services on lines which were still intact. These services carried troops to the battlefront, brought back the wounded to the hospitals (and eventually back to Britain) and moved ammunition to where it was most needed. During the Battle of the Somme the majority of the munitions were moved by rail, although the last few miles to the front were often on road as it was too risky to construct a railway that near to the enemy guns.

Many of the lines operated by the ROD were specially constructed to suit the job at hand but occasionally they were involved with civilian services as well. As the war progressed, tanks became increasingly important and the railways were found to be the ideal active part in the conflict with both sides making use of rail-mounted guns. The Germans had their *Big Bertha* gun and rail-mounted guns such as these shelled Paris, although German forces never reached the city. Similarly, the British mounted naval guns on railway carriages. One example, with a 14-inch calibre, became known as the *Boche-Buster*.

method to move such armoured vehicles quickly around the front. Towards the end of the war, in 1918, a number of tank depots – known as 'tankdromes' – were established and each of these was served by its own railway line.

But the railways also played a more As tourists it is possible to travel by train through the battlefields of the First World War but it is important to remember that the railways, and the railwaymen who worked on them, played a more direct part in the conflict than we might otherwise have thought.

Above: Etaples cemetery, which was positioned to be seen from the train

Again, to the West, on the right-hand side the train passes the village of Morval, about 9 km past Bapaume. There was fierce fighting here in the First World War and a private of the Cheshire Regiment, Thomas Alfred 'Todger' Jones, was awarded the Victoria Cross for singlehandedly taking a series of German positions and disarming more than 100 German soldiers in 1916.

The train continues southwards towards Paris through a landscape that is very much defined by the two world wars that were fought here. However, it is important to remember that this landscape has a history that stretches back much further than the conflicts of the twentieth century.

On the right-hand side, to the West, and about 11 km past St-Léger we pass the town of Bapaume. For centuries, this town was a crossing point between Flanders and the land around Paris and was fortified in the 1300s. However, in the nineteenth century, the fortifications were systematically dismantled. This did not mean that its violent past was behind it. The town was a battlefield in the Franco-Prussian War of the 1870s and was a key objective of the Battle of the Somme in the First World War. As with much of northern France, this town also suffered during the Second World War.

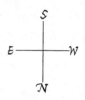

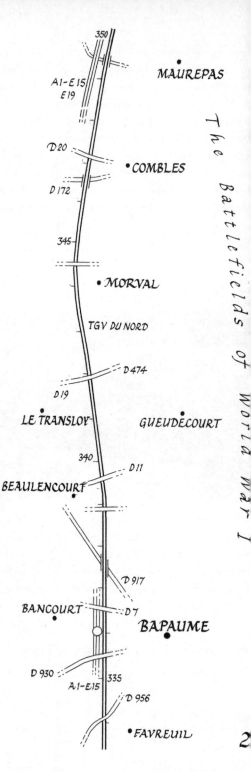

The Battlefields of World War 1

2

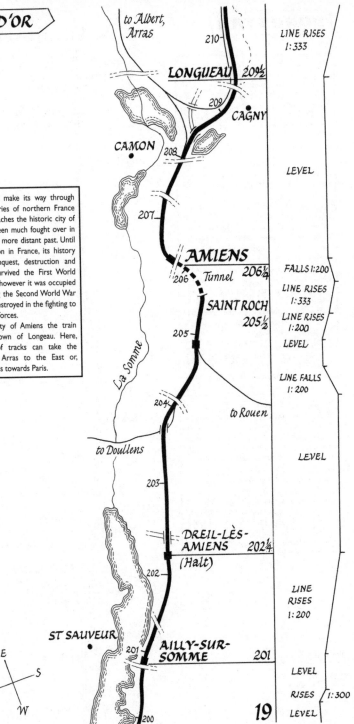

to Albert, Arras

LINE RISES 1:333

LONGUEAU 209½

209

CAGNY

CAMON 208

LEVEL

207

AMIENS 206¼

206 Tunnel

FALLS 1:200

LINE RISES 1:333

SAINT ROCH 205½

LINE RISES 1:200

205

LEVEL

LINE FALLS 1:200

204

to Rouen

La Somme

to Doullens

LEVEL

203

DREIL-LÈS-AMIENS 202¼

(Halt)

202

LINE RISES 1:200

ST SAUVEUR

201

AILLY-SUR-SOMME 201

LEVEL

RISES 1:300

19

LEVEL

200

The train continues to make its way through the jute-making territories of northern France and very soon it approaches the historic city of Amiens. This city has been much fought over in recent years and in the more distant past. Until the Industrial Revolution in France, its history has been one of conquest, destruction and bloodshed. The city survived the First World War almost unscathed, however it was occupied by the Germans during the Second World War and many areas were destroyed in the fighting to liberate it by the Allied forces.

After leaving the city of Amiens the train heads towards the town of Longeau. Here, a complex triangle of tracks can take the traveller off towards Arras to the East or, heading South, continues towards Paris.

E
S
N
W

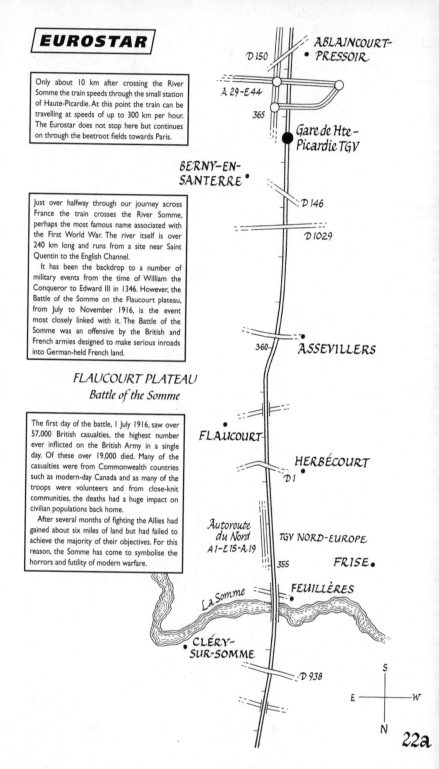

EUROSTAR

Only about 10 km after crossing the River Somme the train speeds through the small station of Haute-Picardie. At this point the train can be travelling at speeds of up to 300 km per hour. The Eurostar does not stop here but continues on through the beetroot fields towards Paris.

Just over halfway through our journey across France the train crosses the River Somme, perhaps the most famous name associated with the First World War. The river itself is over 240 km long and runs from a site near Saint Quentin to the English Channel.

It has been the backdrop to a number of military events from the time of William the Conqueror to Edward III in 1346. However, the Battle of the Somme on the Flaucourt plateau, from July to November 1916, is the event most closely linked with it. The Battle of the Somme was an offensive by the British and French armies designed to make serious inroads into German-held French land.

FLAUCOURT PLATEAU
Battle of the Somme

The first day of the battle, 1 July 1916, saw over 57,000 British casualties, the highest number ever inflicted on the British Army in a single day. Of these over 19,000 died. Many of the casualties were from Commonwealth countries such as modern-day Canada and as many of the troops were volunteers and from close-knit communities, the deaths had a huge impact on civilian populations back home.

After several months of fighting the Allies had gained about six miles of land but had failed to achieve the majority of their objectives. For this reason, the Somme has come to symbolise the horrors and futility of modern warfare.

ABLAINCOURT-PRESSOIR

D 150

A 29 - E 44

365

Gare de Hte-Picardie TGV

BERNY-EN-SANTERRE

D 146

D 1029

360

ASSEVILLERS

FLAUCOURT

HERBÉCOURT

D 1

Autoroute du Nord A1-E15-A19

TGV NORD-EUROPE

FRISE

355

FEUILLÈRES

La Somme

CLÉRY-SUR-SOMME

D 938

S
E — W
N

22a

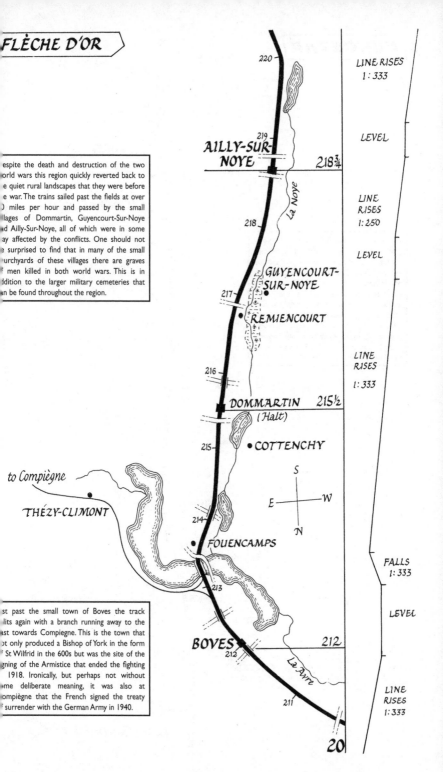

FLÈCHE D'OR

espite the death and destruction of the two
orld wars this region quickly reverted back to
e quiet rural landscapes that they were before
e war. The trains sailed past the fields at over
) miles per hour and passed by the small
llages of Dommartin, Guyencourt-Sur-Noye
d Ailly-Sur-Noye, all of which were in some
ay affected by the conflicts. One should not
e surprised to find that in many of the small
urchyards of these villages there are graves
f men killed in both world wars. This is in
ddition to the larger military cemeteries that
an be found throughout the region.

LINE RISES
1:333

LEVEL

220

219
AILLY-SUR-
NOYE   218¾

La Noye

218

LINE
RISES
1:250

LEVEL

GUYENCOURT-
SUR-NOYE

217

REMIENCOURT

LINE
RISES
1:333

216

DOMMARTIN   215½
(Halt)

215   COTTENCHY

to Compiègne

THÉZY-CLIMONT

214

S

E   W

N

FOUENCAMPS

FALLS
1:333

213

LEVEL

st past the small town of Boves the track
lits again with a branch running away to the
ast towards Compiegne. This is the town that
ot only produced a Bishop of York in the form
f St Wilfrid in the 600s but was the site of the
gning of the Armistice that ended the fighting
1918. Ironically, but perhaps not without
me deliberate meaning, it was also at
ompiègne that the French signed the treaty
f surrender with the German Army in 1940.

BOVES   212
212

La Avre

211

LINE
RISES
1:333

20

LINE
RISES
1:333

81

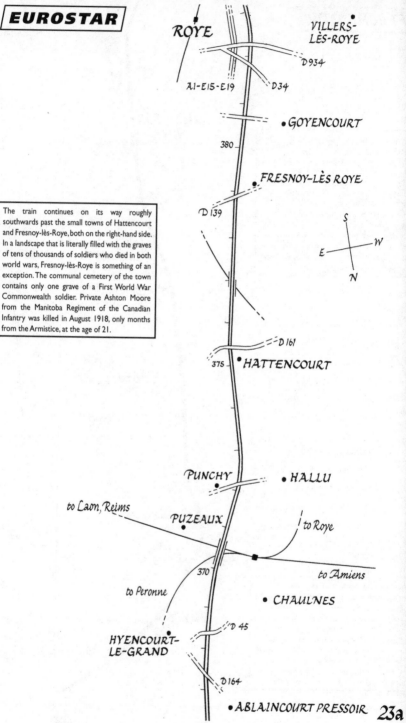

ROYE

VILLERS-LÈS-ROYE

D934

A1–E15–E19   D34

GOYENCOURT

380

FRESNOY-LÈS ROYE

D 139

The train continues on its way roughly southwards past the small towns of Hattencourt and Fresnoy-lès-Roye, both on the right-hand side. In a landscape that is literally filled with the graves of tens of thousands of soldiers who died in both world wars, Fresnoy-lès-Roye is something of an exception. The communal cemetery of the town contains only one grave of a First World War Commonwealth soldier. Private Ashton Moore from the Manitoba Regiment of the Canadian Infantry was killed in August 1918, only months from the Armistice, at the age of 21.

S
E ✛ W
N

D 161

375   HATTENCOURT

PUNCHY   HALLU

to Laon, Reims

PUZEAUX   to Roye

370   to Amiens

to Peronne

CHAULNES

D 45

HYENCOURT-LE-GRAND

D 164

ABLAINCOURT PRESSOIR   **23a**

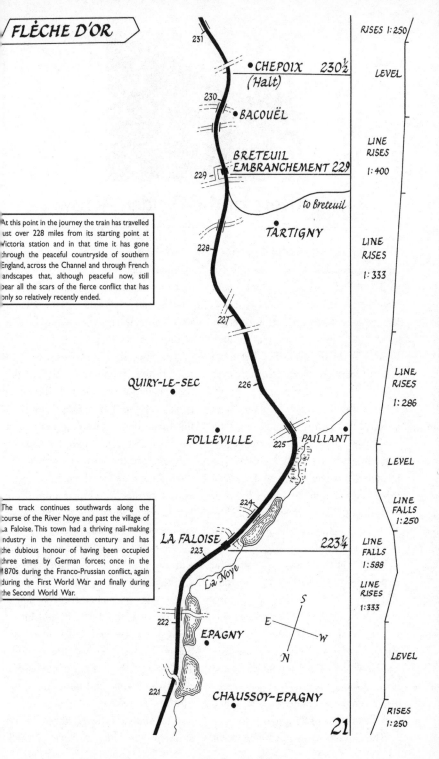

FLÈCHE D'OR

231

• CHEPOIX 230½
(Halt)

230
• BACOUËL

BRETEUIL
EMBRANCHEMENT 229
229

to Breteuil

TÀRTIGNY
228

227

QUIRY-LE-SEC
226

FOLLEVILLE
225 • PAILLANT

224

LA FALOISE
223
La Noye

222

EPAGNY

221

CHAUSSOY-EPAGNY

RISES 1:250

LEVEL

LINE
RISES
1:400

LINE
RISES
1:333

LINE
RISES
1:286

LEVEL

LINE
FALLS
1:250

223¼ LINE
FALLS
1:588

LINE
RISES
1:333

LEVEL

RISES
1:250

S
E   W
N

21

At this point in the journey the train has travelled just over 228 miles from its starting point at Victoria station and in that time it has gone through the peaceful countryside of southern England, across the Channel and through French landscapes that, although peaceful now, still bear all the scars of the fierce conflict that has only so relatively recently ended.

The track continues southwards along the course of the River Noye and past the village of La Faloise. This town had a thriving nail-making industry in the nineteenth century and has the dubious honour of having been occupied three times by German forces; once in the 1870s during the Franco-Prussian conflict, again during the First World War and finally during the Second World War.

The Rivers of the Golden Arrow

The Golden Arrow crossed many rivers on its way from London to Paris. It began with 'Old Father Thames', which would have been crossed by the Grosvenor Bridge at Battersea. There were many rivers and streams that ran through London but by the Victorian period the majority of these had been built over and now flowed underground.

Just after Dunton Green the route crossed the River Darent and then the River Teise, a tributary of the great Kentish river, the Medway. The meandering River Beult was crossed three times as it made its way between Staplehurst and Headcorn before continuing on through the orchards and hop fields of Kent.

The Great Stour was the last of the large rivers encountered by the train and this was crossed twice in the region of Ashford. As the Golden Arrow made its way to Dover Marine only small streams and brooks were encountered.

The SS *Canterbury* was spacious and luxurious, and ensured that passengers arrived on the continent ready for lunch and the final leg of their journey.

The Golden Arrow, or Flèche d'Or

to give it its proper name in French, steamed out of Calais Maritime and crossed the Canal de la Riviere Neuve and then the River Slack, which flows west to the Channel south of Cap Gris Nez.

The Ran de Grigny was crossed just before Wimereux and as the train made its way through Boulogne it passed the broadening mouth of the Liane before crossing a series of small rivulets and then La Canche just south of the town of Etaples. On the right of the route the land was, and still is to this day, very swampy. This land extends to the South and almost submerges la Grande Tingue.

Some miles further along on the journey to Paris the train crossed L'Authie and a whole series of small rivers as it approached Rue. By now it was almost 170 miles from its starting point in London and had reached the Somme Valley at Noyelles-sur-Mer. The town of Abbeville stands astride the River Somme and the route of the Flèche d'Or followed the river all the way to Amiens before it turned south at the town of Ailly-sur-Noye, at which point the River Noye flows back into the Somme.

There are countless small towns and villages scattered through the landscape here. The train would have passed through this landscape at speed and then run

The train was almost at the end of its journey and, once past the town of Chantilly, was only half an hour from Paris. It was here that the suburbs of Paris began to come into view. The Flèche d'Or did not cross the

alongside the River L'Arre at St-Remy-en-l'Eau. After the town of Claremont the line followed the River Brèche before eventually reaching the wide River l'Oise, which flows up through Creil.

mighty River Seine but, once in the heart of Paris at the Gare du Nord, the traveller, their journey complete, would be only a short walk from its romantic banks.

Opposite: The railway bridge at Argenteuil, painted by Claude Monet, 1873–4
Above: Looking down the River Seine towards the limestone cliffs of La Roche Guyon

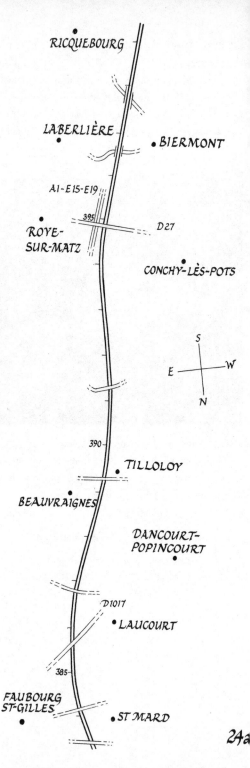

RICQUEBOURG

LABERLIÈRE • BIERMONT

A1-E15-E19

395   D27

ROYE-
SUR-MATZ

CONCHY-LÈS-POTS

390

TILLOLOY

BEAUVRAIGNES

DANCOURT-
POPINCOURT

D1017

LAUCOURT

385

FAUBOURG
ST-GILLES   • ST MARD

24a

While evidence of the two world wars was everywhere in this region it is worth remembering that there is far more to this part of northern France than battles and cemeteries. When travelling through the landscape it is easy to see that this is rich farming country and that livestock and crops are in abundance here. While the coal-producing areas through which we have already passed have suffered greatly with changing economic fortunes, many of the small farms have diversified and are thriving.

More than 80 local farms in the region now actively invite tourists to stay and experience life farming in this region. Although it is possible to stay and to work on the farm tourists are also welcome to stay and relax while enjoying the local food.

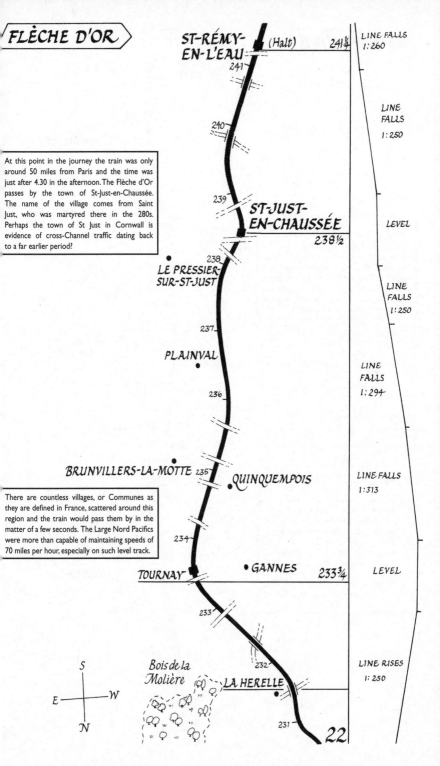

FLÈCHE D'OR

ST-RÉMY-
EN-L'EAU (Halt)
241
241¼

LINE FALLS
1:260

LINE
FALLS
1:250

240

239

ST-JUST-
EN-CHAUSSÉE
238½

LEVEL

At this point in the journey the train was only around 50 miles from Paris and the time was just after 4.30 in the afternoon. The Flèche d'Or passes by the town of St-Just-en-Chaussée. The name of the village comes from Saint Just, who was martyred there in the 280s. Perhaps the town of St Just in Cornwall is evidence of cross-Channel traffic dating back to a far earlier period?

238
LE PRESSIER-
SUR-ST-JUST

LINE
FALLS
1:250

237

PLAINVAL

236

LINE
FALLS
1:294

BRUNVILLERS-LA-MOTTE 235
QUINQUEMPOIS

LINE FALLS
1:313

There are countless villages, or Communes as they are defined in France, scattered around this region and the train would pass them by in the matter of a few seconds. The Large Nord Pacifics were more than capable of maintaining speeds of 70 miles per hour, especially on such level track.

234

GANNES 233¾

TOURNAY

LEVEL

233

232

S

E — W

N

Bois de la
Molière

LA HERELLE

LINE RISES
1:250

231

22

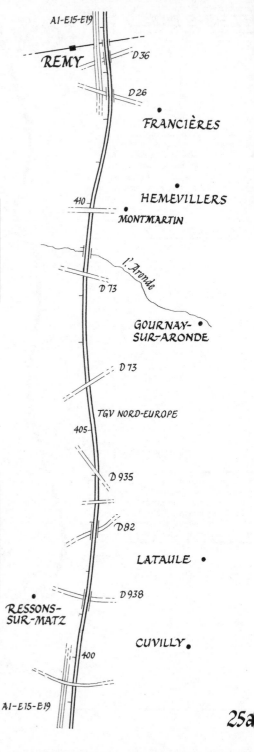

EUROSTAR

A1-E15-E19

REMY

D 36

D 26

FRANCIÈRES

HEMEVILLERS

410

MONTMARTIN

The landscape of Picardy through which the train now runs has a rich cultural tradition that stretches back into the mists of time. Those from this region have distinctive foods and musical instruments, along with their own language of Picard. This region, while so fiercely fought over in the twentieth century, is now peaceful and fertile; crops such as sugar beet, introduced by Napoleon, are still common today.

l'Aronde

D 73

GOURNAY-
SUR-ARONDE

D 73

TGV NORD-EUROPE

405

D 935

We are now less than 100 km from Paris Gare du Nord and the Eurostar is moving through the French countryside at speeds that can reach up to 300 km per hour. The towns flash past us: Cuvilly and Lataule on the right and Ressons-sur-Matz on the left. It was at Ressons-sur-Matz that Nora Saltonstall, who worked as a volunteer with the Red Cross, spent several months in early 1918. She wrote many letters home and described the conditions of life on the front lines.

D 82

LATAULE

D 938

RESSONS-
SUR-MATZ

CUVILLY

400

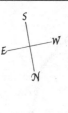

A1-E15-E19

25a

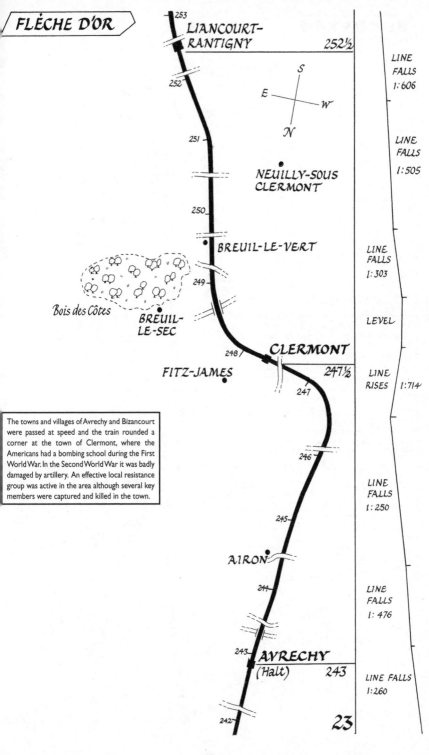

FLÈCHE D'OR

253
LIANCOURT-
RANTIGNY
252½

252

251

NEUILLY-SOUS
CLERMONT

250

BREUIL-LE-VERT

249

Bois des Côtes

BREUIL-
LE-SEC

248
CLERMONT
247½

FITZ-JAMES

247

246

245

AIRON

244

243
AVRECHY
(Halt)
243

242

S
E — W
N

LINE
FALLS
1:606

LINE
FALLS
1:505

LINE
FALLS
1:303

LEVEL

LINE
RISES   1:714

LINE
FALLS
1:250

LINE
FALLS
1:476

LINE FALLS
1:260

23

The towns and villages of Avrechy and Bizancourt
were passed at speed and the train rounded a
corner at the town of Clermont, where the
Americans had a bombing school during the First
World War. In the Second World War it was badly
damaged by artillery. An effective local resistance
group was active in the area although several key
members were captured and killed in the town.

EUROSTAR

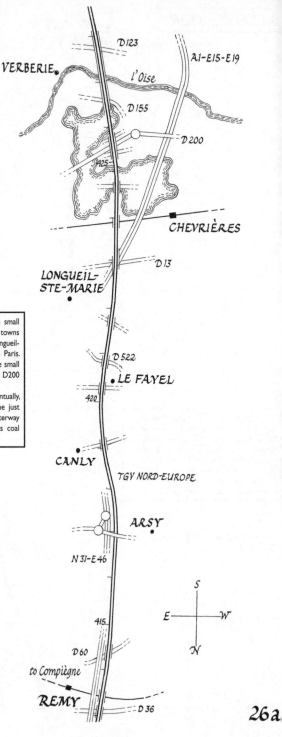

D 123

VERBERIE

l' Oise

A1–E15–E19

D 155

D 200

425

CHEVRIÈRES

D 13

LONGUEIL-
STE-MARIE

The landscape of Picardy is dotted with small villages and as the train speeds past the towns and villages of Remy, Arsy, Canly and Longueil-Sainte-Marie, we make our way towards Paris. The train then passes over the line to the small town of Chevrières before crossing the D200 road and the River Oise.

The Oise rises in Belgium but eventually, after some 300 km, joins the River Seine just north of Paris. It was a vital inland waterway and connected northern France, with its coal reserves, to Belgium and the Netherlands.

D 522

LE FAYEL

420

CANLY

TGV NORD-EUROPE

ARSY

N 31–E 46

S

E — W

N

415

D 60

to Compiègne

REMY

D 36

26a

90

FLÈCHE D'OR

After several hours on the train, and with lunch long gone, the appearance of the town of Chantilly may have prompted the passenger to think of dessert, as it gave its name to the sweet cream used in baking, but it is also the site of France's most famous racecourse. At this point the train was only around 23 miles from Paris, which meant that arrival was imminent.

The train now made its way through the town of Creil, an important railway junction. From here it was possible to reach Compiègne, Beauvais and Saint-Quentin but the Flèche d'Or's route lay ahead of it, on the main line.

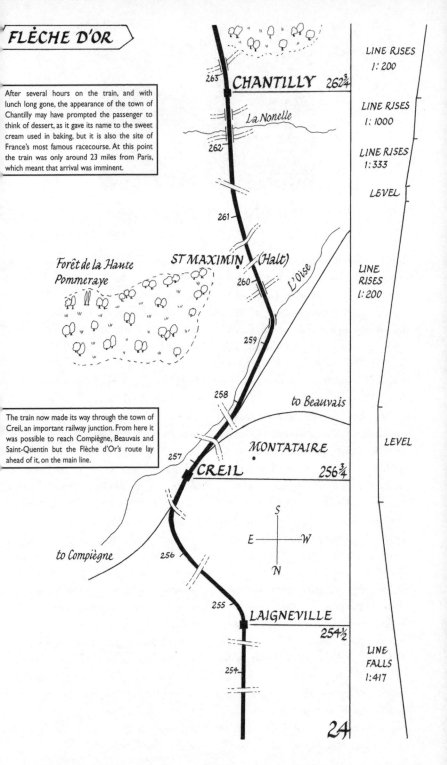

263

CHANTILLY 262¾

La Nonelle

262

261

Forêt de la Haute Pommeraye

ST MAXIMIN (Halt)

260

L'Oise

259

258

to Beauvais

257

MONTATAIRE

CREIL 256¾

to Compiègne

256

255

LAIGNEVILLE 254½

254

LINE RISES 1:200

LINE RISES 1:1000

LINE RISES 1:333

LEVEL

LINE RISES 1:200

LEVEL

LINE FALLS 1:417

24

Further into Europe

Paris may well be our destination but it is by no means the only place we can reach from the Eurostar. Once on the continent, all of Europe opens up before us. While flying has its advantages, travelling by rail gives us the opportunity to experience the landscapes through which we travel on a more intimate level, albeit at 180 mph!

The direct services from London do not just go to Paris. We could go as far as Bourg-Saint-Maurice or Avignon, all on direct Eurostar services. Almost every major city in France is reachable from London via the Eurostar and the domestic French railway's TGV high-speed lines. Within six hours of leaving London we could arrive at Nantes, Dijon or even Marseille on the Mediterranean coast.

Outside of France there are many options available to the traveller. If we turn our attention north, we could, by travelling through Lille, take the Eurostar to Brussels, or change for Ghent or Antwerp in Belgium. By taking the same route we can go even further north and within four hours, be in Rottterdam; one hour later, in Amsterdam. Heading east, it is possible

to change from the Eurostar at Brussels and continue our journey on the ICE (or Intercity Express) to the German city of Cologne on a direct service that would eventually take us all the way to Frankfurt.

But it does not have to stop there. Even Spain is reachable by train with the 'train-hotel' services from Paris, which travel overnight to both Madrid and Barcelona. These trains are fitted out with restaurants, bars and two-bed cabins and provide a more sustainable alternative to flying, although, when travelling overnight, it is important to see the journey simply as part of the whole adventure.

Almost all of Western Europe can be reached quickly by train. The networks of the different countries have all been joined together now and the conflicts where railways were used to move troops, prisoners and refugees are happily a thing of the past. But, if travelling from the United Kingdom, the Eurostar is still the starting point. It can take you, in under two-and-a-half hours, from London to the heart of cosmopolitan Paris.

But it is important to remember that while the speeds may have increased, the ability to travel by rail, quickly and in some luxury, through Europe is no new thing. At its height in the 1930s, the Golden Arrow took you to Paris in comfort and in under five hours. From there, it would have been possible to travel all over Europe on services such as the Orient Express, popularised in the Agatha Christie novel. In its earliest form, in the 1880s, the Express d'Orient took travellers from Paris through Europe to their final destination in Istanbul, Turkey. The service has been discontinued.

Opposite: The ICE (Intercity Express) at Cologne Central station
Above: The Orient Express wagon-lits poster from the 1940s

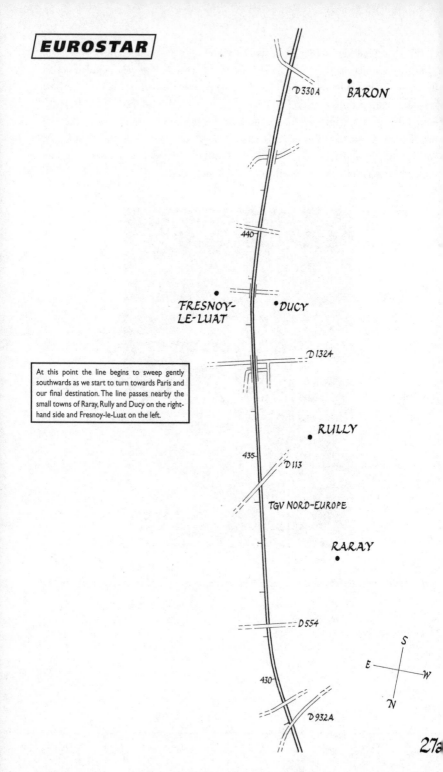

EUROSTAR

D 330 A

•BARON

440

•
FRESNOY-
LE-LUAT

•DUCY

D 1324

At this point the line begins to sweep gently
southwards as we start to turn towards Paris and
our final destination. The line passes nearby the
small towns of Raray, Rully and Ducy on the right-
hand side and Fresnoy-le-Luat on the left.

•RULLY

435

D 113

TGV NORD-EUROPE

RARAY
•

D 554

430

D 932 A

S

E   W

N

27a

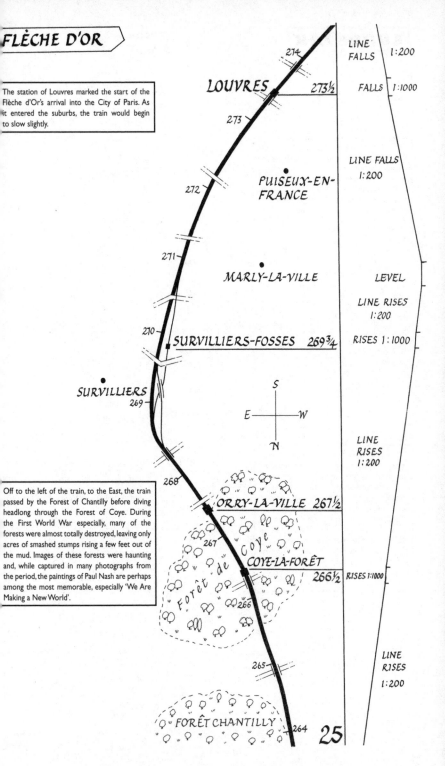

FLÈCHE D'OR

The station of Louvres marked the start of the Flèche d'Or's arrival into the City of Paris. As it entered the suburbs, the train would begin to slow slightly.

LINE FALLS | 1:200

LOUVRES 273½

FALLS | 1:1000

274

273

LINE FALLS 1:200

272

PUISEUX-EN-FRANCE

271

MARLY-LA-VILLE

LEVEL

LINE RISES 1:200

270

SURVILLIERS-FOSSES 269¾

RISES 1:1000

SURVILLIERS 269

S

E — W

N

LINE RISES 1:200

268

Off to the left of the train, to the East, the train passed by the Forest of Chantilly before diving headlong through the Forest of Coye. During the First World War especially, many of the forests were almost totally destroyed, leaving only acres of smashed stumps rising a few feet out of the mud. Images of these forests were haunting and, while captured in many photographs from the period, the paintings of Paul Nash are perhaps among the most memorable, especially 'We Are Making a New World'.

ORRY-LA-VILLE 267½

267

Forêt de Coye

COYE-LA-FORÊT

266½ RISES 1:1000

266

265

LINE RISES 1:200

FORÊT CHANTILLY 264

25

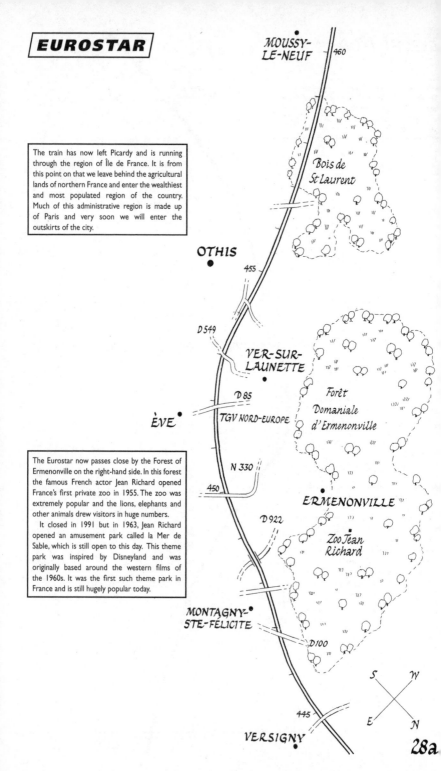

EUROSTAR

MOUSSY-LE-NEUF
460

Bois de St Laurent

The train has now left Picardy and is running through the region of Île de France. It is from this point on that we leave behind the agricultural lands of northern France and enter the wealthiest and most populated region of the country. Much of this administrative region is made up of Paris and very soon we will enter the outskirts of the city.

OTHIS
455

D 549

VER-SUR-LAUNETTE

Forêt Domaniale d'Ermenonville

D 85

ÈVE

TGV NORD-EUROPE

The Eurostar now passes close by the Forest of Ermenonville on the right-hand side. In this forest the famous French actor Jean Richard opened France's first private zoo in 1955. The zoo was extremely popular and the lions, elephants and other animals drew visitors in huge numbers.

It closed in 1991 but in 1963, Jean Richard opened an amusement park called la Mer de Sable, which is still open to this day. This theme park was inspired by Disneyland and was originally based around the western films of the 1960s. It was the first such theme park in France and is still hugely popular today.

N 330

450

ERMENONVILLE

D 922

Zoo Jean Richard

MONTAGNY-STE-FÉLICITE

D 100

S   W

E   N

445

VERSIGNY

28a

96

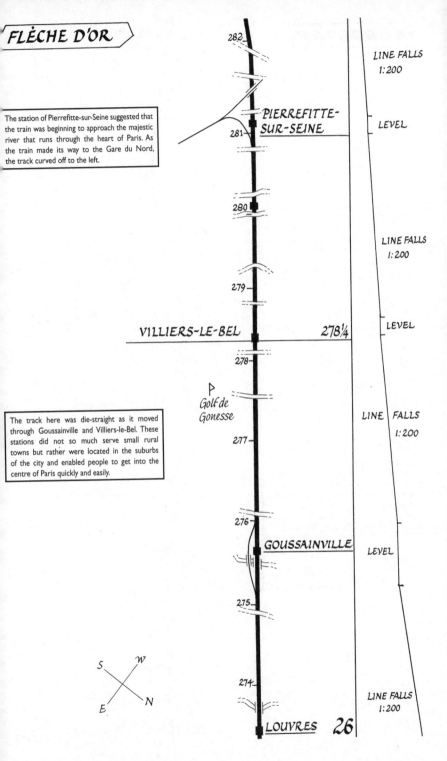

FLÈCHE D'OR

The station of Pierrefitte-sur-Seine suggested that the train was beginning to approach the majestic river that runs through the heart of Paris. As the train made its way to the Gare du Nord, the track curved off to the left.

The track here was die-straight as it moved through Goussainville and Villiers-le-Bel. These stations did not so much serve small rural towns but rather were located in the suburbs of the city and enabled people to get into the centre of Paris quickly and easily.

282

281

PIERREFITTE-
SUR-SEINE

280

279

VILLIERS-LE-BEL   278¼

278

Golf de
Gonesse

277

276

275

274

LOUVRES   26

GOUSSAINVILLE

LINE FALLS
1:200

LEVEL

LINE FALLS
1:200

LEVEL

LINE FALLS
1:200

LEVEL

LINE FALLS
1:200

S   W

E   N

EUROSTAR

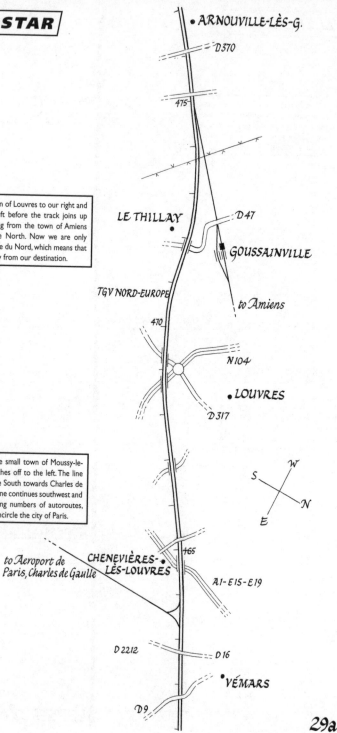

We pass by the town of Louvres to our right and Le Thillay to our left before the track joins up with the line coming from the town of Amiens further back to the North. Now we are only 15 km from the Gare du Nord, which means that we are minutes away from our destination.

About 4 km after the small town of Moussy-le-Neuf the track branches off to the left. The line here runs away to the South towards Charles de Gaulle Airport. Our line continues southwest and crosses over increasing numbers of autoroutes, or motorways, that encircle the city of Paris.

ARNOUVILLE-LÈS-G.

D 370

475

LE THILLAY

D 47

GOUSSAINVILLE

TGV NORD-EUROPE

to Amiens

470

N 104

LOUVRES

D 317

to Aéroport de
Paris, Charles de Gaulle

CHENEVIÈRES-
LÈS-LOUVRES

465

A1 - E15 - E19

D 22.12

D 16

VÉMARS

D 9

29a

The Golden Arrow/Flèche d'Or Pullman poster from 1929 for the improved service by train and boat at 6 hours and 35 minutes

The Gare du Nord

The ultimate destination of both the Golden Arrow and the Eurostar is the beautiful city of Paris. However, in reality, the first place that the traveller by rail from London really encounters is the Gare du Nord. It is from this station that the tourist, businessman or lover sets out to explore the city and, like its counterparts in London, it has a long and interesting history.

Originally the station was opened in 1846 and served the railway company Chemin de Fer du Nord. However, the building was not considered large enough to accommodate all of the traffic coming into the city and rebuilding began in 1860. The original façade of the station was saved from the demolition that accompanied the rebuilding and was shipped, stone by stone, to the city of Lille, where it was reinstated on the station building there, from where it can still be seen.

By 1865 the station had been significantly enlarged and was fully open for traffic. The new façade was bigger and much grander than before and was modelled on a triumphal arch. Architecturally, it was well suited to the pomp and grandeur of the Paris at the time. It was decorated with a series of statues, each one of which represented one of the major cities served by the Chemin de Fer du Nord. These included Brussels, Amsterdam, Frankfurt and Berlin.

However, by the 1890s the station was once again considered to be too small to accommodate all the traffic that went through it. It was once more enlarged and rebuilt. The periodic extension of the station was to continue right up to the 1960s.

The next major overhaul of the station came about as a result of the Eurostar itself. Tracks and platforms were altered once again to accommodate the new high-speed line. The Eurostar speeds into Paris, having passed through Lille – only a short distance from the station frontage that used to grace the Gare du Nord when it first opened over 160 years ago. One traveller, arriving in Paris on the Golden Arrow, described seeing the station as he neared his journey's end as nothing more than 'A black dome'. Its massive train shed certainly seems to swallow up with apparent ease all

the trains that terminate there. But it is also more than just a station: it carries with it the symbols of the far-flung cities it joins together and stands for the connections which the railways made possible. While it is a terminus, one of the six major termini of the city, it is also a gateway. A gateway not only to the city, but also to the continent beyond it.

Opposite: Crates containing items destined for the Great Exhibition at Crystal Palace, London, 1851
Above: Gare du Nord, Paris in 1903. Within 100 years, trains would arrive direct from London in under 2 hours and 30 minutes

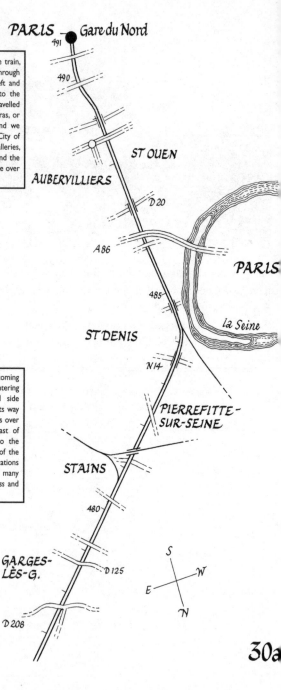

PARIS — Gare du Nord
491

The city of Paris is all around us and the train, travelling more slowly now, passes through the communes of Aubervilliers to the left and St Ouen on the right before pulling into the platform at the Gare du Nord. We have travelled a total of 491 km from London St Pancras, or in English terms just over 300 miles, and we have now arrived into the heart of the City of Light. All of Paris is before us now – the galleries, museums, boulevards and restaurants – and the journey from London has taken only a little over two-and-a-quarter hours.

490

ST OUEN

AUBERVILLIERS

D 20

A 86

PARIS

485

la Seine

ST DENIS

N 14

We now enter the suburbs of Paris, first coming through the commune of Stains before entering Pierrefitte-sur-Seine. On the right-hand side the River Seine can be seen as it winds its way through the heart of the city. This river is over 770 km long and rises in the Northeast of France near Dijon before emptying into the English Channel at le Havre. The banks of the Seine are among the most picturesque locations in Paris and have been the backdrop to many films including Jean-Luc Godard's *Breathless* and *The Pink Panther*.

PIERREFITTE-
SUR-SEINE

STAINS

480

GARGES-
LÈS-G.

D 125

S

W

E

N

D 208

30a

As the train rounds the corner, the Seine can be seen for the first time. It curves gracefully off to the right as the train is swallowed up by the city, which appears almost untouched by the conflicts that have raged all around it over the past century. Paris is undoubtedly among the most cosmopolitan places in the world, although its long history has been marked by unrest and conflict.

The approach to the centre of Paris in the inter-war period would have been far from dull as the train moved past tenements, coal yards, railway sidings and the backs of grand buildings. Along the sides of buildings were advertising hoardings for pastis and wines, which would perhaps have inspired the traveller as they thought about what to do once they arrived in the City of Light.

The train would pull in to the platform at 5.35, all being well, a perfect time for an aperitif; 288 miles had been travelled from London to this point. The channel had been crossed on a steam ship dedicated to the service and only open to those who carried a ticket for the Golden Arrow. The Flèche d'Or, as the French named it, was designed to be luxurious and elegant, a perfect way to enter one of the most luxurious and elegant cities in the world.

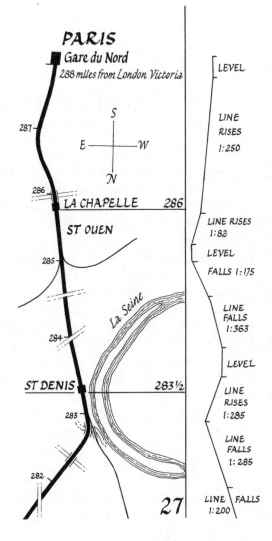

PARIS
Gare du Nord
288 miles from London Victoria

287

S
E — W
N

286
LA CHAPELLE 286
ST OUEN
285

La Seine

284

ST DENIS 283½
283

282

27

LEVEL

LINE RISES 1:250

LINE RISES 1:82
LEVEL
FALLS 1:175

LINE FALLS 1:363

LEVEL

LINE RISES 1:285

LINE FALLS 1:285

LINE FALLS 1:200

The Locomotives of the Golden Arrow

The Golden Arrow was a prestige service and, as such, it demanded the finest of locomotives to haul it non-stop to the coast. In the years directly before the introduction of the service in 1929 the Southern Railway made used the King Arthur class 4-6-0 locomotives to haul the boat trains from the capital. However from 1926, as the trains got larger and heavier, the more powerful Lord Nelson class 4-6-0s were used.

The Lord Nelson class of locomotives was seen by many in the 1930s as 'the arrow-head' and one writer described the moment that the locomotive set off from London in September 1930.

'Now she coughs loudly thrice, opening her lungs to the line. There is a lurch as of tremendous strength unleashed.'

They were designed by Richard Maunsell, the then Chief Mechanical Engineer of the Southern Railway, and first appeared in 1926. They had six driving wheels each 6' 7" in height and the weight of the engine and tender was over 140 tons. These powerful engines were more than capable of hauling the Golden Arrow even though the train weighed more than 450 tons in total.

Many other locomotives hauled the Golden Arrow after the war including the Bulleid designed Merchant Navy class 4-6-2s which were affectionately known as 'spam cans' due to their distinctive bodywork.

In France the Flèche d'Or was generally hauled by the larger and more powerful Nord 'Super Pacific' locomotives. These engines became famous for their power and strength even in England and they weighed in at a substantial 153 tons. They could carry seven tons of coal, as opposed to the Lord Nelson's five, and carried considerably more water in the tender.

The French 'loading gauge' was, and still is, much larger than that in England. This meant that the bridges, platforms and line side buildings allowed for a far larger locomotive to pass by them. It was this that paved the way for such a large and powerful locomotive to be used on the continent.

After the Second World War there were many different types of locomotives used to haul the service. But, with the end of steam a romantic chapter of railway history was lost forever. For many, the idea of such a prestigious service as the Golden Arrow being hauled by an electric locomotive took away all the glamour and beauty. However, the style and performance of the Eurostar has caused many to think again.

On the fifth anniversary of the opening of the Eurostar – in 1999 – it stands alongside the Golden Arrow, the prestigious cross-channel service that ran from 1929 until 1972

Acknowledgments

Our thanks go to Michael Bunn and the members of the SNCF Society for providing invaluable information about the routes through France and to the press office at *Eurostar* headquarters in London for information regarding the route in England.

Picture Credits

The publisher would like to thank the following for providing images for this book:

Alamy pages 22, 43, 46, 47, 58, 84, 85, 99
Getty Images pages 23, 26, 32, 33, 37, 44, 77, 100, 105
Mary Evans pages 8, 9, 14, 15, 36, 40, 42, 44, 59, 70, 101
Mirrorpix pages 27, 71
RIBA pages, 41
Science & Society Picture Library pages 19, 64, 65, 93